ISS I0052045

Dediu Newsletter

Author: Michael M. Dediu

Monthly news, reviews, comments and suggestions for a better and wiser world

Vol. **2**, Nr. **10 (22)**, 6 September **2018**

DERC Publishing House

Tewksbury (Boston), Massachusetts, U. S. A.

For subscriptions please use the contact form at www.derc.com

Published and printed in the
United States of America
On the Great Seal of the United States are included:
E Pluribus Unum (Out of many, one)
Annuit Coeptis (He has approved of the undertakings)
Novus Ordo Seclorum (New order of the ages)

Dediu, Michael M.

Dediu Newsletter Vol 2, Number 10 (22), 6 September 2018
Monthly reviews, comments and suggestions for a better and
wiser world

ISSN 2475-2061
ISBN 978-1-939757-75-3

Preface

August 2018 was nice and warm, end of summer, with preparations for the starting of school.

Many good news from research in science, medicine, technology, and other areas. Also, a wedding of Austrian Foreign Minister Karin Kneissl and Wolfgang Mailinger, with some guests. We added a page with humor, for some healthy relaxation.

In this 10th newsletter of the second volume, the 22nd in total, we included the most relevant news, in a balanced approach, usually directly from the source, to help the general public better understand the realities around us. We included also several nice photos - I thank my wife for her photo assistance. Being well and correctly informed is a sine qua non requirement for everybody, in order to make the right decisions for the future.

Enjoy this newsletter and be optimist!

Michael M. Dediu, Ph. D.

Tewksbury (Boston), U. S. A., 6 September 2018

16 April 2016, from the north side of the Boston Common (1634, 50 acres, central public park in downtown Boston and the oldest city park in the USA (hosted British troops in 1765-1783)), looking southeast to buildings on Tremont St. Just behind the white apartment building (center left), the Boston Opera House (1928, capacity 2,677, sumptuous, vaulted, rededicated in 1980 as a home for the Opera Company of Boston, with many Boston Ballet performances) is located on Washington St at Avenue de Lafayette.

Table of Contents

Paris, Île de la Cité: the oldest public clock in France, built in 1370 with a mechanism from 1334, adorned with the statues of Piety (left) and Justice (right), on the front of the Tour de l'Horloge (1350 – 1353, 47 m high, at the north-east corner of La Conciergerie, the Palace of French Kings from 950 until 1358 when they moved to Louvre), at the corner of the Palais de Justice, on Boulevard du Palais at the junction with Quai de l'Horloge, in the 1er Arrondissement, 350 m north-west of Notre Dame (1345).

United States of America

(Population 324.4 M, rank 3, growth 0.7%. Free: 89 of 100).

Reports: WILL Research Director Will Flanders, Ph.D., looked at the relationship between test scores and the number of non-teachers in a school district, per pupil spending in a district, and teacher pay, in a new report titled Money for Nothing: The Relationship Between Various Types of School Funding and Academic Outcomes. None of these factors seem to be linked to higher student test scores.

The website DietDetective.com, founded by the director of the Hunter College NYC Food Policy Center, has been rating the "best" and "worst" airline foods every year since 2009, assigning them "Health Scores," from 0 (lowest) to 5 (highest), as well as reporting on calories, personal favorites, suggestions about what to order (and what to avoid), and other considerations such as how sustainable the foods are and how committed the airlines seem to be about providing healthier fare. Here are some highlights from the 2017-18 investigation, which evaluated the economy-class food aboard 12 domestic airlines flying within the U.S. Delta and Virgin America (now owned by Alaska Air) tied as "healthiest" (score of 4.0), followed by Air Canada and JetBlue (tied at 3.75), Alaska Air (3.5), United (2.75), American (2.5), Frontier Air (2.25), Southwest (2.0), Spirit (1.75), and Allegiant Air (1.75). Hawaiian Airlines ranked lowest (1.0).

9 August is National Book Lovers Day.

Reports: Cybercriminals committed identity theft, which affected 14.7 millions of Americans.

For years, cybercriminals have been experimenting with new ways to steal and extort money from their victims. In the last few years, the biggest trend is cryptocurrency.

People ask authorities to arrest the cybercriminals.

10 August 2018. Reports: The Pentagon has released a 15-page report outlining a framework for the establishment of the U.S.

Space Force, which would become the sixth military branch. Efforts include an "acceleration" of space technology, the creation of a space-development agency, and a pool of "space experts" and "space warfighting professionals." The division would be responsible for protecting against hypersonic weapons, as well as attacks on communications satellites, and the Pentagon's missile-warning systems.

14 August 2018. Reports: More Democrats have a favorable view of socialism (which is just one small step away from Communism) than those who have a favorable view of capitalism, according to a Gallup poll released Monday, 13 August.
Of Democrats and those who lean Democrat surveyed, only 47% had a favorable view of capitalism, down from 56% in 2016. 57% said they viewed socialism favorably, which is within the margin of error (+\- 3 percent) from the 58% of Democrats who viewed socialism favorably in 2016.
By contrast, 71% of Republicans had a favorable view of capitalism — a number that is within the margin of error from the 68% who viewed it favorably in 2016. Only 16% of Republicans said they viewed socialism favorably, which is also within the margin of error from the 13% of those who viewed it favorably when Bernie Sanders (I-Vt.) was on the campaign trail seeking the Democratic nomination for president, two years ago.

19 August 2018. Reports: Advocacy groups are sounding the alarm that a quick surrender by House Republicans on 2019 spending bills in the coming weeks, could ruin the morale of grass-roots activists the GOP will need for the closing stretch of the midterm campaign season. Lawmakers are intent on avoiding a government shutdown next month, but those who want fiscal discipline say a more orderly spending process won't mean anything if it leads to bloated spending bills, that can win bipartisan support in the Senate, rather than leaner bills that advance GOP priorities.
Dr. Ben Carson, the secretary of Housing and Urban Development (HUD), wants to pare back previous administration era housing regulations, that he says do not do enough to address the real driver of housing costs: zoning regulations. On Monday, 13 August, Dr. Carson announced that he was looking to revise the

2015 Affirmatively Furthering Fair Housing (AFFH) rule, which requires local governments to perform extensive (and expensive) reviews on how concentrated their neighborhoods were along class and racial lines, and then to develop action plans to create more "balanced and integrated living patterns." Local governments that failed to fulfill either requirement would be cut off from a number of federal housing grant programs. Dr. Carson said on Monday that he wants to replace the 2015 AFFH with new rules that focus on increasing the overall supply of housing.

The four richest counties in the United States (and nine of the top 20) are all suburbs of Washington, D.C. Loudoun County, Virginia takes the #1 spot with a median household income of $125,900. That is more than double the median household income for the entire country. While small businesses are struggling to make ends meet, Washington, D.C., is a boomtown for the politically connected. Every year, hundreds of Capitol Hill staffers, and members of Congress, leave their jobs to make a fortune selling influence on K Street. Fifty special interest groups spent more than $716 millions to lobby the federal government in 2016. American taxpayers paid $3.27 trillions to fund the federal government, while top lobbyists got paid $2.6 billions telling Congress how to spend it.

Reports: The Strategic Petroleum Reserve was established in the 1970s, after the U.S. economy was paralyzed by an oil embargo. As recently as 2011 it contained 727 M barrels in caverns along the Texas and Louisiana coasts.

Reports: U.S. hospitals have been closing at a rate of about 30 a year, according to the American Hospital Association, and patients living far from major cities may be left with even fewer hospital choices, as insurers push them toward online providers like Teladoc, and clinics such as CVS's MinuteClinic. The next year to 18 months could see a further increase in shutdowns, with the risks coming following years of mergers and acquisitions.

Reports about rough and not so good justice. Some of the biggest lawsuits pending in federal courts today involve products that are completely legal, heavily regulated, and used by millions of consumers. But none of that matters when private lawyers join forces with public entities to sue for big money.

Reports about big nanny who is watching everybody. Former Homeland Security Director Michael Chertoff argues in a new book that, unless our structures change, the main casualty of the big-data growth won't be our privacy—it could be our autonomy.

Reports on how the United States landed in a debt "danger zone". The interaction of public and private debt in the United States reduced economic growth about 0.43% per year between 2009 and 2014, a new study suggests. In addition, growth declined an additional 0.4% due solely to the high level of debt.
– Ohio State University

Reports on midterm: the latest projection by Height Capital Markets has the Democrats winning control of the House of Representatives by a 5 to 15 seat margin in November's midterm elections. The firm expects the Senate to stay in GOP control, and prevent legislation that would allow Medicare to negotiate drug prices, establish a drug price gouging enforcer, or require manufacturers to justify to HHS their price increases.

25 August 2018. Xinhua: A senior U.S. Navy official said Friday, 24 August, that the U.S. 2nd Fleet will expand its operation space past the Arctic Circle and reach close to Russia.
"A new 2nd Fleet increases our strategic flexibility to respond - from the Eastern Seaboard to the Barents Sea" (north of western Russia), Chief of Naval Operations John Richardson said aboard the aircraft carrier George H.W. Bush, which is currently at Norfolk in the U.S. state of Virginia. "Second Fleet will approach the North Atlantic as one continuous operational space, and conduct expeditionary fleet operations where and when needed," Richardson said.
The U.S. 2nd Fleet, which traditionally covers the Western Atlantic, was deactivated in 2011, after the Pentagon decided it was too expensive to sustain a fleet to cover an area that has remained largely peaceful. Richardson in May announced that the Pentagon will reconstitute the 2nd Fleet, and with his latest signal Friday, the fleet is set to play a bigger role in the U.S. Navy. Vice Admiral Andrew

Lewis, commander of the 2nd Fleet, said that the expansion of the fleet is an embodiment of the national defense strategy released earlier this year, which stressed "great power competition."

Former Deputy Secretary of Defense Bob Work told U.S. media that, to bring U.S. warships to Russia's doorstep, will curb U.S. ability to maneuver its submarines in open water, which can threaten the U.S. Navy.

Reports: In order to bring down drug prices, one must address the problems of government overreach, including the public funding of prescription drugs, drug patents, and the web of regulation engendered by the Food and Drug Administration — a combination of factors affecting both the supply and demand sides of the equation.

Reports: Fiscal conservatives and many others thought they had a good chance this year to trim billions in farm subsidies that flow to wealthy commodity growers. Despite years of methodical planning and lobbying, their efforts during the 2018 farm bill were thwarted by some of the very lawmakers who were thought to be aligned with their interests. "This wasn't a matter of being beaten. We were blocked," the director of federal affairs for the National Taxpayers Union, told POLITICO. "Let's have the fight. I'm fine with losing on the floor. But to not even have a discussion is selling taxpayers short," the director added.

The coalition pushing to rein in farm subsidies is a disparate bunch: It includes libertarians seeking spending cuts, and free-marketers like the Heritage Foundation. Although these strange allies have long tried to limit farm payments, the coalition thought this farm bill cycle could be their moment. Not only is Congress controlled by Republicans, many of whom express a distaste for big government, but the White House also included proposals in its budgets that would cut off subsidies for farmers with high incomes.

Reports: Rural America voted for President Trump in a 3-to-1 margin in hopes that a newcomer to the White House could defray stagnant economic conditions. Now, as the president's trade policies start to squeeze the farming and manufacturing communities, who cheered his election two short years ago, these Americans are left to wonder whether the man they sent to Washington still has their backs. Trump has publicly expressed support for "zero tariffs" in trade negotiations, so actions the administration takes to the contrary are increasingly perplexing, given how strong their economic damage is on his base. Data show that the steel and aluminum tariffs imposed by the administration could cost as many as 400,000 American jobs, far outstripping any jobs purportedly saved by protectionist policies. And as a 25% tariff goes into effect today on $16 B worth of additional Chinese goods, the 1.7 million Americans whose jobs rely on these goods have cause to wonder whose aims the administration's trade tactics serve.

New York Public Library (1895, 1908, 87 branches (Carnegie libraries (Andrew Carnegie (1835-1919))), 53 millions of books and other items, the 2nd largest public library in the United States (behind the Library of Congress), and the fourth largest in the world.)

Reports: With some U.S. farm products getting stopped by retaliatory tariffs, the Trump administration is prepared to begin its emergency agriculture plan right after Labor Day in a "three-pronged approach" that will initially include about $6 B in aid. Farmers "cannot pay their bills with simple patriotism," Agriculture Secretary Sonny Perdue declared. Some farm groups, however, are cautioning the spending won't make up for losses from the trade clashes.

Reports: Despite controlling the Senate, the House, and the White House, Senate Republicans have failed to keep their biggest promises.

31 August 2018. Reports: President Trump has disregarded an offer from the EU to eliminate tariffs on cars if the U.S. did the same, declaring it "not good enough" as European "consumer habits are to buy their cars, not to buy our cars." In the interview with Bloomberg, he also said the EU is "almost as bad as China, just smaller," then told aides he supports tariffs on an additional $200 B in Chinese goods as early as next week. He doesn't regret appointing Jerome Powell as Fed Chairman, and said Jeff Sessions' job is safe until at least the November elections. Trump is also thinking about linking capital gains taxes to inflation, and is seeking to eliminate pay raises for civilian federal employees next year. He'll also withdraw from the World Trade Organization if it doesn't "shape up."

Reports on Madison (WI) School District: alarming difference between spending and graduation rates going up from 2008 to 2017, white the American College Testing (ACT) results going badly down:

	Graduation rates (%)		ACT Reading (%)		ACT Mathematics (%)	
	White	Non-white	White	Non-white	White	Non-white
2008	88	49 – 56	79	37 – 54	75	29 - 48
2017	91	72 – 76	69	12 – 24	66	8 - 21

Reports: STDs continue rapid rise in U.S., setting new record, CDC says.

Life expectancy declines seen in U.S. and other high-income countries.

A poll conducted by NPR found that 71% of Americans say they have "not very much" or "no confidence" in Congress.

Currently, 2.3 M are held in U.S. correctional facilities — more people than live in the entire state of New Mexico — costing over $80 B/year. For that outlay, families are divided, youthful potential squandered, and millions of dollars wasted by the U.S. injudicious approach to justice.

Reports: The First Step Act, a prison reform bill, passed the House in May on a 360 to 9 vote.

Reports: In a recent survey, an astounding 47% of college graduates did not even know that U.S. Senators are elected to 6-year terms, and U.S. Representatives to 2-year terms. This is alarming, but perhaps not surprising. For many decades, our K-12 schools and universities have failed to teach young Americans the basics of American history and government, including basic knowledge of the U.S. Constitution. This poses a danger to the future of free government.

Puerto Rico: (Population 3.6 M, rank 134, decrease 0.1%; an unincorporated territory of the United States, located in the northeast Caribbean Sea, 1,600 km southeast of Miami, Florida.).
9 August 2018. Reports: Puerto Rico has reached an agreement with creditors to restructure bonds backed by a portion of its sales tax known as Cofinas, solidifying a planned restructuring of roughly $18 B in debt. The agreement, which requires court approval, would mark the biggest consensual debt settlement negotiated with creditors since the island entered a court-supervised bankruptcy last year.

United Nations.   There are 195 officially recognized countries. Around 44,000 people work for the United Nations. There is a wide range of jobs: Researchers, IT-specialists, lawyers, experts on finance and administration, or translators work at the New York headquarters, at the official locations, or at specialized agencies. More than half of the UN's workforce is employed in the field, in projects of humanitarian aid, or on peace missions.
18 August 2018. The President of Russia sent a message to UN Secretary-General Antonio Guterres expressing his deepest condolences on the death of former UN Secretary-General Kofi Annan (from Ghana).

China, Japan, and neighbors

China: (Population 1.4 B, rank 1, growth 0.4%. Freedom House reports for 2018: Not Free (15 of 100)). 6 August 2018. Reports: Over the weekend, 5 August, China accused the U.S. of blackmail, and said its most recent retaliatory tariffs on $60 B of U.S. goods showed rational restraint.

6 August 2018. Reports: The U.S. has the upper hand on China, President Trump said at a rally outside Columbus, Ohio, declaring that Chinese stocks are down, and weakening that nation's bargaining power. The duties are working "big time," he added, suggesting they will allow paying down "large amounts of the $21 T in debt that has been accumulated", while reducing taxes for Americans. China's state media responded, accusing Trump of "starring in his own carefully orchestrated street fighter-style deceitful drama", and warning it was prepared for a "protracted war."

7 August 2018. Reports: Since 2015, China has outspent the U.S. by $24 B in 5G infrastructure, potentially creating a growth that will be difficult to catch up with, according to a new study by Deloitte. China has built 350,000 new cell sites, while the U.S. has built fewer than 30,000 in the same time frame. 5G would support connected infrastructure in cities, including driverless cars, and make it possible for people to stream high-bandwidth video.

8 August 2018. Reports: China's exports growth unexpectedly accelerated in July, despite fresh American tariffs, as its closely watched surplus with the U.S. dipped only slightly to $28.09 B last month from a record $28.97 B in June. The two sides have also shown no signs of letting up, with the U.S. finalizing plans overnight to begin collecting 25% tariffs on another $16 B in Chinese goods - across 279 product lines - on Aug. 23.

8 August 2018. Reports: "China doesn't want to close its doors to Apple, despite the trade conflict, but if the U.S. company wants to earn good money in China, it needs to share its development dividends with the Chinese people, or face anger and nationalist sentiment amid the ongoing trade war," warned the state-backed People's Daily. The article originally appeared in another state-backed publication, Global Times, last week.

8 August 2018. Reports: While it did not provide a reason, China has denied Walt Disney's request to screen Christopher Robin in the country, Reuters reports. The decision has revived online discussion, as censors have in the past targeted Winnie the Pooh, although the country also limits the number of foreign-made films allowed in to 34 a year.

9 August 2018. Reports: Bending to demands from China's aviation regulator, airlines including Delta, United, American and Hawaiian, have amended their systems to list only Taipei's airport code and city, but not the name Taiwan. They also changed references for Hong Kong and Macau, former European colonies that are now part of China, but are run largely autonomously.

Reports: The Bai ethnic group is one of the 56 ethnic groups officially recognized in China. Of the 1,858,063 Bai people, 80% live in concentrated communities in the Dali Bai Autonomous Prefecture in Yunnan Province, southwest China.

13 August 2018. Reports: Google's core services such as search, Gmail and You Tube remain blocked for Chinese citizens.

15 August 2018. Reports: China's J-20 stealth jet fighter may have electro-optical sensor system similar to the F-35.

15 August 2018. Reports: China has filed a complaint with the World Trade Organization, saying that U.S. tariffs on solar products are distorting the global photovoltaic market, and hurting its trade interests. The country claims its makers are benefiting not from subsidies but from healthy competition.

15 August 2018. Vladimir Putin met with Yang Jiechi, member of the Politburo of the Communist Party of China's Central Committee responsible for foreign policy. Various bilateral issues were discussed, as well as details of the upcoming visit to Russia by President of the People's Republic of China, Xi Jinping.

President of Russia Vladimir Putin: Comrade Yang Jiechi, dear friends. It is a pleasure to see you. I would like to start our meeting by noting that our relations are developing as planned, everything is going according to our plan. This is largely due to the proactive stance of our reliable, good friend President Xi Jinping.

Please convey my best wishes to him. We are looking forward to his visit. It will take place in Vladivostok this September, and then together we will take part in the Vladivostok Economic Forum.

Last year bilateral trade amounted to $87 billions. In the first half of this year alone it increased by 50%, and this year it will likely reach $100 billions. I know that you have already held fairly detailed talks today with Mr. Patrushev. I am very pleased.

Member of the Politburo of the Communist Party of China Central Committee Yang Jiechi: Your Excellency Mr. President, I am very grateful to you for meeting with me and my colleagues today. I will pass along your best wishes to President Xi Jinping by all means. Allow me to also convey to you President Xi's best wishes and warm regards. Your Excellency Mr. President, in June you paid a state visit to Beijing and then attended the Qingdao Summit. In July of this year, you took part in the BRICS Summit together with President Xi Jinping. During these events, you had a detailed conversation with President Xi Jinping on a broad range of issues. All of your meetings were highly important, and added a powerful new impetus to the development of bilateral relations.

Following the generous invitation, President Xi Jinping will attend the forthcoming Eastern Economic Forum in Vladivostok. A regular top-level meeting of the two leaders will also take place.

We believe the forthcoming meeting will be a major event in the foreign policies of China and Russia. There is no doubt that the next Russia-China summit will be crowned with great success. We would also like to wish success to the forthcoming Eastern Economic Forum. There will be many opportunities for top-level bilateral meetings on the sidelines of international events before the end of the year. It is important for us to fully prepare for these meetings.

You were absolutely right in saying that bilateral trade and economic ties are continuously growing both in quantity and quality, and we can expect trade to reach $100 billion.

At the instruction of the leaders of the two countries, Mr. Patrushev and I conducted a regular round of consultations on strategic security. Our consultations focused on practical matters, and were highly productive. We are very grateful to Russia for the warm reception and excellent organization of our stay. I have already invited Mr. Patrushev to attend a regular round of consultations on strategic security next year.

Mr. Putin, thank you once again for receiving us today.

Vladimir Putin: For our part, we remember the truly warm and friendly reception we enjoyed in China last June, almost like family,

I would say. We will do our best to offer the same to President Xi Jinping. I do not know if we succeed, but we would like to do this very much, in both substance and form.

Reports: China's military focuses on artificial intelligence. China's missile destroyers are prepared to guard aircraft carriers.

20 August 2018. Reports: Six days of public hearings on proposed U.S. duties on Chinese imports of up to 25% will begin today in Washington. "USTR's proposed tariffs on an additional $200 B dramatically expands the harm to American consumers, workers, businesses, and the economy," the U.S. Chamber of Commerce said in written testimony for the hearing. Mid-level Trump administration officials and their Chinese counterparts will likely meet later this week in Washington to discuss their escalating trade war.

20 August 2018. Xinhua: President Xi Jinping has called for efforts to comprehensively strengthen the leadership of the Communist Party of China (CPC), and the Party building, in the country's armed forces, to ensure a solid political guarantee for the building of a strong military. Xi, also general secretary of the CPC Central Committee, and chairman of the Central Military Commission (CMC), made the remarks at a CMC meeting on Party building, which was held from Friday, 17 August, to Sunday, 19 August, in Beijing.

Noting that strengthening CPC leadership and Party building in the military is a requisite for advancing the "great new project" of Party building, and the building of a strong country with a strong military, Xi said the whole military should comprehensively implement the Thought on Socialism with Chinese Characteristics for a New Era and the spirit of the 19th CPC National Congress.

The Party's thinking on strengthening the military for the new era must be fully implemented, Xi said. Also, the absolute Party leadership over the armed forces must be upheld, the full and strict Party governance must be exercised, and the military's war preparedness and combat capability must be highlighted, Xi said.

Since the 18th CPC National Congress, the CPC Central Committee and the CMC have been working on building the military and keeping hold of it from a political perspective, Xi said, citing a conference on the army's political work convened in 2014 in Gutian Township, Fujian Province.

Comprehensive and profound changes regarding the Party leadership and Party building in the military have taken place, giving a strong political underpinning for the historic achievements and changes in the cause of building a strong military, Xi said.

Xi noted that the CPC leadership and Party building are essential to the construction and development of the military, and matter to the success of the cause of building a strong army, and the enduring peace and stability of the Party and the country.

He said the primary task is to uphold the absolute CPC leadership over the armed forces. The political building of the Party should be intensified to make sure that the whole military resolutely upholds the authority of the CPC Central Committee and its centralized, unified leadership, and resolutely obeys the command of the CPC Central Committee and the CMC.

Efforts should be made to arm the military with the Thought on Socialism with Chinese Characteristics for a New Era and the Party's thinking on strengthening the military for the new era, Xi said.

Also, measures should be taken to ensure that all kinds of work are placed under the unified leadership of the Party committees and all important issues are discussed and decided by the Party committees, he stressed, adding that the system for the Party's leadership over the military should also be improved.

To fulfill the primary duty of war preparedness and combat capability, more efforts are needed in improving the system of Party organizations in the armed forces and strengthening their leadership, organizational and executive capacity, according to Xi.

Xi highlighted the crucial role and responsibility of Party committees of units at or above corps-level in the military's Party organization system, and called on them to take a clear political stand and a firm political stance, maintain a correct political direction, hold a strong political conviction, improve their political capability, and ensure that they stay politically strong.

Stressing the prominent importance in cultivating cadres and talent, Xi called for efforts in training high-caliber cadres who are loyal to the Party, have moral integrity, and demonstrate a keen sense of responsibility, and gathering talent in various areas who are committed to building a strong military and winning combat.

The training of talent in joint operations command, new combat forces, high-tech innovation, and high-level strategic management should be improved, said Xi. He also urged efforts to improve Party conduct and combat corruption in the armed forces.

"The anti-corruption fight must be carried forward with firmness, and there will be no deviation," said Xi.

At the meeting, Xu Qiliang and Zhang Youxia, both members of the Political Bureau of the CPC Central Committee and the CMC's vice chairmen, raised their requirements on implementing the spirit of Xi's speech, and strengthening the Party leadership and Party building in military. CMC members Wei Fenghe, Li Zuocheng, Miao Hua, and Zhang Shengmin also attended the meeting.

Reports: U.S. would need anti-missile satellite mega-constellation to counter China's hypersonic weapons.

23 August 2018. Reports: A fresh round of U.S. tariffs on $16 B worth of Chinese imports started at midnight, prompting Beijing to retaliate with its own levies on American goods worth the same amount. The world's two largest economies (the second being under Communist government), which are in the midst of trade talks, have now imposed tit-for-tat duties on a combined $100 B of products since early July, with more in the pipeline. Economists estimate that every $100 B of imports hit by tariffs would reduce global trade by around 0.5%.

24 August 2018. Reports: Mid-level trade talks between the U.S. and China ended without any formal signs of progress, although Chinese officials said they plan to keep the lines of communication open. Sources indicated the two sides mainly swapped talking points, without getting any detailed negotiations. Today, representatives from the U.S., European Union, and Japan plan to meet in Washington to extend talks on how to leverage the World Trade Organization, and other ways pressure can be exerted on China.

25 August 2018. Xinhua: President Xi Jinping on Friday, 24 August, called for strengthening the centralized and unified leadership of the Communist Party of China (CPC) over advancing law-based governance in all areas. Xi, also general secretary of the CPC Central Committee, chairman of the Central Military Commission, and head of the Commission for Law-based Governance of the CPC Central Committee, made the remarks while presiding over the first meeting of the commission.

Efforts should be made to unswervingly promote socialist rule of law with Chinese characteristics and enable the rule of law to better play its role of guarantee for a solid foundation, stabilized expectations and long-term interests, Xi said. Li Keqiang, Li Zhanshu and Wang Huning, members of the Standing Committee of the Political Bureau of the CPC Central Committee and deputy heads of the commission, attended the meeting.

Documents including the commission's working rules and its work priorities in 2018 were adopted at the meeting.

The rule of law and the Party's leadership over law-based governance in all areas need to be further strengthened in order to uphold and develop socialism with Chinese characteristics, Xi said. The CPC Central Committee has since the 18th CPC National Congress in 2012 made a series of major decisions on law-based governance in all areas, which are the fundamental rules for law-based governance and must be adhered to and steadily developed on a long-term basis, he said. With this year's work priorities made clear, Xi called on relevant authorities to formulate a plan on building the rule of law in China, fully implement and enforce the Constitution, ensure legislation is sound, strengthen the building of a government based on the rule of law, deepen judicial system reform, advance efforts to build a society based on the rule of law, and train judicial personnel. Xi said the commission should focus its energy on top-level design, take the initiative to design the overall thinking and decide on the major tasks for building the system of the socialist rule of law with Chinese characteristics, and do the planning and scientific decision-making on key issues concerning the law-based governance in all areas.

Reports: China rules the web technology in service of the state. China's proposed 'no child tax' means a change from "first forced abortions", to "pressured into pregnancy". Who needs democracy when you have data? China rules using data, AI, and internet surveillance. Google employees are organizing to protest the company's secret, censored search engine for China. It appears that a new Comintern for the new era is being developed. China's interest in becoming a 'polar great power', was officially proclaimed at Xi Jinping's 2014 speech in Hobart. An economics professor was expelled for 'politically harmful' expressions, including estimate of staggering cost to maintain the Communist Party apparatus.

27 August 2018. Xinhua: Chinese President Xi Jinping has called on all members of the Communist Party of China (CPC) to learn from three late comrades from a research institute, stressing patriotism. The three comrades -- Huang Qun, Song Yuecai and Jiang Kaibin -- who worked for the 760 Research Institute of the China Shipbuilding Industry Corporation, sacrificed their lives to protect a national experimental platform during Typhoon Rumbia, when it passed through Dalian, a coastal city of northeast China's Liaoning province, on Aug. 20. All Party members should draw strength from the three late comrades, have firm ideals and convictions, remain true to their original aspiration, keep their mission firmly in mind, perform their duty scrupulously, be loyal to the Party, and make contributions to the country, said Xi, who is also general secretary of the CPC Central Committee, and chairman of the Central Military Commission.

28 August 2018. Reports: President Trump said he's rejecting overtures from China to negotiate, as he tries to achieve a less "one-sided" trade policy. "They want to talk... but it's just not the right time to talk right now, to be honest." Chinese officials reportedly raised the prospect of suspending talks last week, until after U.S. congressional elections in November.

28 August 2018. Reports: China this week is considering scrapping its birth restrictions, with the draft civil code set to be completed by 2020. Couples are limited to two children at present, after rules were relaxed from the notorious one-child policy that was in force for 37 years, from 1979 to 2016.

Reports: Sand is used in all concrete buildings, paved roads, glass, silicon chips, etc. Now there is the issue of running out of it. China is the world's top producer and consumer of construction sand, and home to the world's biggest sand mine— Lake Poyang, China's largest freshwater lake, which is being badly damaged by dredging. China is also the world leader in using sand to create artificial land — a power it has used to build the Spratly Islands in the South China Sea into a military outpost, creating a major flashpoint with its neighbors and the U.S.

Reports: Google is on the verge of making a huge mistake with China arrangement to accept censorship.
China signals end to child birth limits by 2020 at latest.

VOA: Authorities force Chinese citizens to renounce belief in Christianity.

4 September 2018. Reports: Chinese President Xi Jinping has pledged $60 B in financing for projects in Africa, in the form of assistance, investment and loans, following a pledge of another $60 B at the previous FOCAC summit in South Africa three years ago. Some Western officials have blamed China for engaging in "debt trap" diplomacy through the financing, with several even accusing Beijing of pursuing colonial exploitation in Africa, through the Belt and Road initiative.

4 September 2018. Reports: China is exploring a merger between two of the nation's three wireless carriers, amid a race with the U.S. over 5G technology, Bloomberg reports. State-run China Unicom and China Telecom both trail China Mobile in scale, but their joint market value is almost $80 B. A deal could speed up the government's 5G ambitions, because a combined company could make the necessary investments more easily than separately. premarket.

Hong Kong. (Population 7.3 M, rank 104, growth 0.8%. Partly Free: 61 of 100). Reports: Hong Kong and Macau students will face compulsory military training at top mainland Chinese university for first time.

Reports: Pro-Democracy Party criticizes Communist Party 'brainwashing' in Hong Kong school textbooks.
Mainland Chinese university bars two Hong Kong human rights lawyers from teaching regular course there.

Macau (Population 622 K, rank 167, growth 1.7 %.)

Taiwan: (Population 23.6 M, rank 56, growth 0.3%. Free, 91 of 100). 6 August 2018. Reports: Cybercriminals sent a computer virus at Apple supplier Taiwan Semiconductor Manufacturing, which could delay some upcoming iPhone shipments, as the chip supplier warned of a $255 M hit to revenue.
People ask for the arrest of cybercriminals.

21 August 2018. Reports: Taiwan has pledged to fight China's "increasingly out of control" behavior, after Taipei lost another ally to Beijing. El Salvador has become the third country to

switch allegiances to China this year, as President Xi warns that the issue of unification cannot be put off indefinitely. Taiwan now has formal relations with only 17 countries worldwide, many of them small, less developed nations in Central America and the Pacific.

Japan (Population 127.5 M, rank 11, decrease 0.2%. Free, 96 of 100). 10 August 2018. Reports: Japan returned to solid growth in the April-June quarter, with the economy expanding at an annualized pace of 1.9%, following a mild contraction in Q1, which ended the longest stretch of growth in 28 years. Economists expect the trend to continue on the back of higher wages and consumer spending, unless trade conflicts with the U.S. worsen.

31 August 2018. Reports: Japan's defense ministry is requesting its biggest budget increase in five years at 5.3 T yen ($48 B). A large chunk of the spend is for Lockheed Martin's Aegis Ashore ballistic missile defense system, to shield the entire Japanese archipelago. Besides threats from North Korea, Japan has come under pressure to buy more military equipment from the U.S., which defends Japan under a postwar security pact, and stations some 54,000 military personnel there.

Japan: the north side of Mount Fuji (3,776 m, 1707 last eruption) seen from Kawaguchiko (Lake Kawaguchi, 6 km^2, 830 m elevation,

100 km south-west of Tokyo, 17 km north of Mount Fuji), with a branch of a blossomed cherry.

Afghanistan: (Population 35.5 M, rank 40, growth 2.5%. Not free: 24 of 100).

South Korea: (Population 50.9 M, rank 27, growth 0.4%. Free, 82 of 100). 8 August 2018. Reports: The Samsung Group will invest 25 T won ($22 B) over three years on artificial intelligence, 5G, auto-tech components, and its biopharmaceutical business, with the bulk of spending earmarked for Samsung Electronics. The news comes amid new research that Galaxy S7 smartphones are vulnerable to cybercriminals' attacks (the devices were previously thought to be immune to a security vulnerability known as Meltdown). People are asking the authorities to arrest the cybercriminals.

North Korea: (Population 25.4 M, rank 52, growth 0.5%. Not free: 3 of 100). 13 August 2018. Reports: North and South Korea have agreed to hold a summit in Pyongyang by September, in what would be the third meeting this year between North Korea's Kim Jong Un and South Korea's Moon Jae-in. Although a fixed agenda for the coming summit meeting has not been set, South Korean officials are expected to discuss ways to keep alive planning for more economic cooperation, and to negotiate ways of easing military tensions on the inter-Korean border.

20 August 2018. Reports: China's President Xi Jinping is expected to visit Pyongyang in September, to attend the celebrations for the 70th anniversary of North Korea's founding. Rumored in Beijing for some time, the visit was reported in Singapore's The Straits Times at the weekend, although it has still to be confirmed by the Chinese government. The visit would be the first to North Korea by a Chinese president since Xi's predecessor, Hu Jintao, went to Pyongyang in 2005.

22 August 2018. Reports: North Korea is continuing to develop its nuclear program, according to the International Atomic Energy Agency, despite an agreement reached in June between Washington and Pyongyang to denuclearize the Korean Peninsula. Asked about the report, a White House National Security Council

spokesman referred to national security adviser John Bolton's assertion earlier this month that President Trump was holding diplomatic doors open for Kim Jong-un.

Vietnam (Population 95.5 M, rank 15, growth 1%. Not free, 20 of 100).

Laos (Population. 6.8 M, rank 106, growth 1.5%. Not free: 12 of 100).

Cambodia (Population 16 M, rank 71, growth 1.5%. Not Free 31 of 100).

Mongolia (Population 3 M, rank 137, growth 1.6%. Free 85 of 100)

Nepal: (Population 29.3 M, rank 48, growth 1.1%. Partly free 52 of 100).

Russia, Switzerland, Eastern Europe

Russia: (Population 143.9 M, rank 9, growth 0%. Not free: 20 of 100). 10 August 2018. Reports: Russian Prime Minister Dmitry Medvedev has reportedly warned the U.S. that sanctions it plans to impose against Moscow. could be treated as a declaration of an economic war. "And it would be necessary, it would be needed to react to this war economically, politically, or, if needed, by other means. And our American friends need to understand this."

History: 75 years ago - the Battle of Kursk (5 July 1943 – 23 August 1943 (49 days), 500 km south of Moscow), which was one of the decisive battles of the WWII (in Russia Great Patriotic War), involving over four millions of soldiers on both sides, German and Russian, as well as nearly 70,000 pieces of ordnance, over 13,000 tanks and self-propelled guns, and 12,000 combat aircraft. With its victory in the battle, the Red Army seized the strategic initiative in the war once and for all.

Switzerland: (Population 8.4 M, rank 99, growth 0.9%. Free: 96 of 100).

Austria: (Population 8.7 M, rank 98, growth 0.3%. Free: 95 of 100). 18 August 2018. The President of Russia briefly visited the Austrian city of Graz on his way to Berlin, for talks with Federal Chancellor of Germany Angela Merkel. Mr. Putin was a guest at the wedding of Austrian Foreign Minister Karin Kneissl and Wolfgang Mailinger. Vladimir Putin gave the newlyweds presents, danced with the bride, and had a brief conversation with Austrian Chancellor Sebastian Kurz, who also attended the celebration.

Poland: (Population 38.1 M, rank 37, decrease 0.1%. Free: 89 of 100). Reports: "The fall of the Berlin Wall makes for nice pictures," said Poland's Lech Walesa, the charismatic Gdańsk electrician who co-founded Solidarność (Solidarity), the first independent trade union behind the Iron Curtain. "But it all started in the shipyards." Labor Day is a good time to remember Walesa, who turns 75 in September, and 35 years ago, in 1983, won the Nobel Peace Prize. He's the most important labor leader of our era.

Together, Walesa, Solidarity workers, Western leaders, and Pope John Paul II defied Soviet totalitarianism in Poland, playing a decisive role in ending the Cold War, and expanding human freedom. American students should know Walesa's name. Unfortunately, on the history and civics portion of the 2014 National Assessment of Educational Progress, "the Nation's Report Card," most U.S. kids scored below "proficient." History instruction is clearly lagging in the U.S. schools.

Croatia: (Population 4.1 M, rank 129, decrease 0.6%. Free: 87 of 100).

Finland: (Population 5.5 M, rank 116, growth 0.4%. Free: 100 of 100). 22 August 2018. The President of Russia held talks in Sochi, Russia, with President of the Republic of Finland, Sauli Niinistö, who is in Russia on a working visit.
Beginning of conversation with President of Finland, Sauli Niinistö.
President of Russia Vladimir Putin: Mr. President, colleagues,
I am very happy to welcome you in Russia.
Quite recently, I had the pleasure of visiting Helsinki, where we met with the President of the United States. I would like to thank you once again for your hospitality, and for the extremely good organization of our work. But we also have many issues of mutual interest in the context of our bilateral relations. This includes the further expansion of economic ties. On the whole, we are satisfied with how this situation is developing. Besides, we have many border issues, as well as cooperation in this area and cultural ties.
We know about your idea to organize an Arctic Council summit. We are also ready to discuss this, and I can say right away that we are ready to take part in this work.
We are very happy to see you, Mr. President.
President of Finland Sauli Niinistö (In Russian.): Spasibo bolshoye. You know, Sochi and sunshine are almost one and the same thing. It is very pleasant to come here.
Vladimir Putin (In Finnish.): Kiitos. [Thank you.]
Sauli Niinistö: Indeed, it was a great honor for Finland to provide a venue for your meeting with the President of the United States. And we believe and hope that this meeting will produce a good result, including in disarmament. As neighboring countries, we have many

common matters of interest. You have already mentioned the economy. And thank you for your promise to take part in Arctic affairs, which we already mentioned.

As neighbors, we also share the environment. We have favorable opportunities in this area, and it is possible to expand our currently positive cooperation for the sake of nature conservation.

Thank you for your invitation. We are enjoying our stay in Sochi.

24 August 2018. The President of Russia had a telephone conversation with President of Finland Sauli Niinistö.

Vladimir Putin warmly congratulated President of the Republic of Finland, Sauli Niinistö, on his 70th birthday.

Romania (Population: 19.6 M, rank 59, decrease 0.5%. Free: 84 of 100)

Moldova: (Population: 4 M, rank 132, decrease 0.2%. Partly Free: 62 of 100).

Belarus: (Population: 9.4 M, rank 93, decrease 0.1%. Not Free: 20 of 100). 22 August 2018. Vladimir Putin met with President of Belarus, Alexander Lukashenko, in Sochi.

Bulgaria: (Population: 7 M, rank 105, decrease 0.7%. Free: 80 of 100).

Slovenia: (Population: 2 M, rank 148, growth 0.1%. Free: 92 of 100).

Hungary: (Population: 9.7 M, rank 91, decrease 0.3%. Free: 76 of 100)

Ukraine: (Population: 44.2 M, rank 32, decrease 0.5%. Partly free: 61 of 100).

Latvia: (Population: 1.9 M, rank 150, decrease 1.1%. Free: 87 of 100).

Lithuania: (Population: 2.8 M, rank 141, decrease 0.6%. Free: 91 of 100).

Estonia: (Population: 1.3 M, rank 155, decrease 0.2%. Free: 94 of 100).

Serbia: (including Kosovo: Population: 8.7 M, rank 97, decrease 0.3%. Free: 76 of 100).

Kosovo ((Disputed: recognized by 110 countries, and not recognized by Serbia, Russia, and others) Population: 1.8 M, Partly free: 52 of 100).

Turkey: (Population 80.7 M, rank 19, growth 1.2%. Partly free: 38 of 100). 6 August 2018. Reports: In response to financial sanctions the U.S. announced against two members of the Turkish government, President Erdogan has ordered the freezing of the "American justice and interior ministers' assets in Turkey, if there are any."

10 August 2018. Reports: Turkey's problems are spilling over into the greater market, following reports that the ECB is concerned over the impact of a weak lira on European banks, especially BBVA, UniCredit, and BNP Paribas. Data from the BIS also showed the currency, which plunged 13.5% overnight to an all-time low against the dollar, will weigh on banking exposure internationally. For now, Turkish President Recep Erdogan said he will stand up to the pressure, stating "don't forget, if they have their dollars, we have our people, our God."

10 August 2018. The President of Russia had a telephone conversation with the President of the Republic of Turkey, Recep Tayyip Erdogan. The presidents discussed the current state and future prospects of trade and economic cooperation between the two countries, and positively assessed the implementation of joint strategic projects, primarily in energy.
The schedule of contacts at different levels was reviewed.

Turkey's lira pulled back from an overnight record low of 7.24 to the dollar after Pres. Erdogan reiterated his opposition to raising interest rates and said the lira's recent free-fall was the result of a foreign plot and did not reflect Turkey's economic fundamentals.

13 August 2018. Reports: Turkey's lira pulled back from an overnight record low of 7.24 to the dollar, after Pres. Erdogan reiterated his opposition to raising interest rates, and said the lira's recent free-fall was the result of a foreign plot, and did not reflect Turkey's economic fundamentals.

15 August 2018. Reports: Turkey has responded to U.S. tariffs with retaliatory duties on U.S. passenger cars, alcohol, tobacco, cosmetics and other products. Tariffs on cars are set to rise by 120%, and those on made-in-the-U.S. alcoholic drinks by 140%, alongside a 60% increase on tobacco products. The move comes amid increasing fears of contagion from Turkey.

17 August 2018. Reports: President Trump said the U.S. "will pay nothing" to Turkey for the release of the detained American pastor.

20 August 2018. Reports: Turkey's President Erdogan declared Saturday,18 August, that his country would not be intimidated by the U.S., as a high court rejected another appeal to free pastor Andrew Brunson, who has been held for almost two years on terrorism charges. "Some people threaten us with economy, sanctions, foreign currency exchange rates, interest rates, and inflation. We know your trickeries, and we will defy you." The bitter feud between Ankara and Washington triggered a trade row last week.

20 August 2018. Reports: Gunshots rang out at the U.S. embassy in Ankara this morning as shots fired from a vehicle hit a window in a security cabin, but caused no casualties. It comes as the Trump administration rejected an effort to tie the release of the pastor with relief for Turkey's Halkbank, which faces billions of dollars in U.S. fines, and follows an agreement from Qatar to help the Turkish economy weather a currency rout.

24 August 2018. Vladimir Putin received Turkish Foreign Minister Mevlüt Çavuşoğlu, and Turkish Minister of Defense, Hulusi Akar, in the Kremlin.
The meeting was also attended by Head of Turkey's National Intelligence Organization, Hakan Fidan.
Taking part in the meeting on the Russian side were Foreign Minister Sergei Lavrov, Defense Minister Sergei Shoigu and

Special Presidential Representative for the Syrian Settlement, Alexander Lavrentyev.

President of Russia Vladimir Putin: Colleagues, friends,

I am pleased to welcome you in Moscow. I know that you have already held consultations with your Russian partners in the Foreign Ministry, the Defense Ministry, and representatives of special services. Relations with Turkey are growing deeper and more substantive, not to mention the regular contacts with President Erdogan. I would like to speak about the deepening cooperation in the economy and on resolving a number of regional issues, including urgent ones like the Syrian crisis. Thanks to our countries' efforts and the involvement of other concerned states, I mean Iran in particular, as well as our cooperation with the United Nations, European countries and the United States, we have made significant progress towards settling the Syrian crisis. I know that you have also discussed other matters of mutual interest today. I am glad to see you and to hear your assessment of where we are now, and what we have to do in the short and longer term to promote our relations.

Foreign Minister Mevlüt Çavuşoğlu: Mr. President,

First of all, we would like to thank you for receiving us.

Your good friend Mr. Erdogan sends his greetings and best regards, and expects your visit to Istanbul soon. You have plans to go to a seafood restaurant. It is true that our relations at the presidential level are very good, and this drives us to promote relations at our level as well. Today our foreign ministers held talks. Our colleagues discussed regional issues at their respective levels. All cooperation matters were discussed. It is very important for us, not only at the state level, but in the regional context as well.

Greece: (Population 11.1 M, rank 82, decrease 0.2%. Free: 84 of 100). 20 August 2018. Reports. Greece may come back to normal, as nearly a decade of external financial help, and the nation's third bailout comes to an end. Athens will now be able to tap financial markets to fund its activities, marking the closure of the European sovereign debt crisis after Portugal, Ireland and Spain came back from the brink.

Republic of North Macedonia: (Population 2 M, rank 147, growth 0.1%. Partly Free: 57 of 100).

Albania: (Population 2.9 M, rank 139, growth 0.1%. Partly free: 68 of 100).

Cyprus: (Population 1.1 M, rank 159, growth 0.8%. Free: 94 of 100).

Kazakhstan (Population 18.2 M, rank 64, growth 1.2%. Not free: 22 of 100). 12 August 2018. The President of Russia has arrived in Aktau to attend the Fifth Caspian Summit, being held in the Republic of Kazakhstan.
The presidents of Azerbaijan, Iran, Kazakhstan, Russia and Turkmenistan discussed key aspects of cooperation in the Caspian region across various areas. They also reviewed the implementation of the decisions taken during previous meetings of the heads of state of the 'Caspian five'.
Following the summit, the presidents signed the Convention On the Legal Status of the Caspian Sea, a document which has been in development since 1996. Additionally, a number of intergovernmental documents were signed during the meeting.
12 August 2018. The President of Russia met with President of the Republic of Kazakhstan Nursultan Nazarbayev. The two leaders held a separate talk following the Fifth Caspian Summit in Kazakhstan.

Armenia: (Population 2.9 M, rank 138, growth 0.2%. Partly free: 45 of 100). 16 August 2018. The President of Russia had a telephone conversation with Prime Minister of Armenia, Nikol Pashinyan, at the Armenian side's initiative.
The discussion focused on topical issues of the bilateral agenda, as well as cooperation within common integration associations, including the Collective Security Treaty Organization.

Azerbaijan: (Population 9.8 M, rank 90, growth 1.1%. Not free 14 of 100)

Uzbekistan: (Population 31.9 M, rank 44, growth 1.5%. Not free: 3 of 100).

Kyrgyzstan (Population 6 M, rank 112, growth 1.5%. Partly free, 37 of 100).

Tajikistan: (Population 8.9 M, rank 96, growth 2.1%. Not free, 11 of 100).

Turkmenistan: (Population 5.7 M, rank 113, growth 1.7%. Not free, 4 of 100). The President of Russia received President of Turkmenistan, Gurbanguly Berdimukhamedov, at his Sochi residence in Russia. During the meeting, the leaders discussed key issues of developing bilateral cooperation in the political, trade, economic, scientific, educational, cultural and humanitarian areas, as well as major regional issues.

United Kingdom, Canada, South America

United Kingdom: (Population: 66.1 M, rank 21, growth 0.6%. Free: 95 of 100). 28 August 2018. Reports: The U.K. can still make a success of Brexit if it tumbles out of the EU without a deal, according to the Prime Minister. "I've said right from the beginning that no deal is better than a bad deal." Trade Secretary Liam Fox echoed the comments in Singapore, where he is making the case for the U.K.'s accession to the Comprehensive & Progressive Agreement for Trans-Pacific Partnership.

Ireland: (Population: 4.7 M, rank 123, growth 0.8%. Free: 96 of 100)

Canada: (Population: 36.6 M, rank 38, growth 0.9%. Free: 99 of 100). 28 August 2018. Reports: The Canadian Foreign Minister will travel to Washington today to continue trade negotiations. "We'll give them a chance to have a separate deal, or we could put it into this," President Trump declared, adding that the "simplest deal is more or less already made." "We will only sign a new NAFTA that is good for Canada and good for the middle class," a spokesman replied in a statement.

4 September 2018. Reports: "There is no political necessity to keep Canada in the new NAFTA deal," President Trump tweeted on Saturday, 1 Sep. "If we don't make a fair deal for the U.S. after decades of abuse, Canada will be out. Congress should not interfere with these negotiations or I will simply terminate NAFTA entirely & we will be far better off." While the president has the power to terminate the pact with six months' notice, it isn't clear if such a decision could withstand the many legal challenges that are likely to surface.

Mexico: (Population: 129.1 M, rank 10, growth 1.3%. Partly Free: 65 of 100). 23 August 2018. Reports: Mexican President-elect Andrés Manuel López Obrador will hold off auctioning any new oil blocks for at least two years, and plans to amend laws to bolster the dominant role of state oil company Petróleos Mexicanos, WSJ reports. The incoming administration won't propose changes to

Mexico's Constitution, which was amended in 2013 to allow for private investment in oil and gas, but will use its majority in Congress to twist the hydrocarbons law.

28 August 2018. Reports: Mexico and the U.S. reached a trade agreement.

Chile: (Population: 18 M, rank 65, growth 0.8%. Free 94 of 100).

Colombia: (Population: 49 M, rank 29, growth 0.8%. Partly free 64 of 100).

Argentina: (Population: 44.2 M, rank 31, growth, 1%. Free: 82 of 100). 14 August 2018. Reports: Argentina's move to boost its 7-day Leliq rate by 5%, to 45%. The central bank vowed to keep the key interest rate at that level until at least October. Late Monday, Argentina's peso erased its loss sustained earlier in the day. The government also canceled its daily dollar auction, and said it will gradually eliminate its holdings of short-term notes.

30 August 2018. Reports: Argentina's peso fell 7.5% against the dollar on Wednesday, 29 August, bringing losses to nearly 50% over the past year, after President Macri asked the IMF to speed up delivery of a $50 B bailout package. It was the largest one-day decline since the currency was allowed to float in 2015, prompting central bank interventions and concern that the third-largest Latin American economy (after Brazil and Mexico) may not meet its debt obligations.

31 August 2018. Reports: The Argentine peso has overtaken Turkey's lira to become the worst performer in foreign exchange markets in 2018, after a 0.15% rise in interest rates on Thursday, 30 August, failed to halt the decline of the currency. That takes the peso's year-to-date decline against the dollar to 51.7%, past the 42.9% drop the lira is having. Other emerging market currencies are also in pain, like the South African rand, and India's rupee.

Brazil (Population: 209.2 M, rank 6, growth 0.8%. Free, 79 of 100). 7 August 2018. Reports: After briefly closing the entry point, Brazil has reopened its northern border with Venezuela to those fleeing economic and political turmoil. With a severe crisis plaguing the country, more than 1 M people have left Venezuela since 2015.

10 August 2018. Reports: Radware has identified a cybercriminals' hijacking campaign aimed at Brazilian bank customers. Targeting a customer's IoT devices, the cybercriminals modify the DNS server settings in the routers of Brazilian residents, and redirects their DNS requests to a cloned website, to garner their personal information.

People ask for the arrest of cybercriminals.

Peru: (Population: 32.1 M, rank 5, growth 1.2%. Free: 72 of 100)

Cuba: (Population: 11.4 M, rank 42, growth 0.1%. Not free, 15 of 100).

Bolivia: (Population: 11 M, rank 83, growth 1.5%. Partly free 68 of 100).

Paraguay: (Population: 6.8 M, rank 107, growth 1.3%. Partly free 64 of 100).

Panama: (Population: 4.1 M, rank 131, growth 1.6%. Free: 83 of 100).

Venezuela: (Population: 32 M, rank 43, growth 1.3%. Not free: 30 of 100). 6 August 2018. Reports: At least one explosion rocked a military event where Venezuela's President Maduro was giving a speech on Saturday, 4 August. Six people have been arrested for the failed assassination attempt involving drones carrying explosives. It comes as the nation's economy suffers under a fifth year of a severe crisis, that has sparked malnutrition, hyperinflation and mass emigration.

20 August 2018. Reports: Ahead of a major currency overhaul today, when Caracas will start issuing new banknotes after slashing five zeroes off the crippled bolivar, President Maduro detailed other measures he hopes will pull Venezuela out of crisis. They include hiking the minimum wage by over 3,000%, boosting

the corporate tax rate, and increasing highly-subsidized gas prices in coming weeks.

30 August 2018. Reports: With more than 1.6 M Venezuelans fleeing the petrostate since 2015 - an outflow equal to the Mediterranean refugee crisis - South American governments are meeting this week to try to manage the continental disaster together. Officials from Colombia, Peru and Ecuador will discuss measures to prevent epidemics, harmonize identification requirements, and share the burden of relief, as the crisis worsens amid plunging oil output and hyperinflation.

Guyana: (Population 777K, (rank 165, grows 0.6%). Free: 74 of 100).

Trinidad and Tobago: (Population 1.3 M, (rank 153, grows 0.3%). Free: 81 of 100).

Nicaragua: (Population 6.2 M, (rank 110, grows 1.1%). Partly Free: 47 of 100).

France, Germany, and neighbors

France: (Population 64.9 M, rank 22, growth 0.4%. Free: 90 of 100). 10 August 2018. The President of Russia had a telephone conversation with the President of the French Republic, Emmanuel Macron. The two leaders exchanged views on the ongoing developments in Syria, and praised the operation carried out by Russia and France in July, to deliver and distribute humanitarian aid in the Syrian province of Eastern Ghouta.

Vladimir Putin stressed the importance for the international community to keep up its efforts to facilitate the restoration of Syria's social and economic infrastructure, as well as to help refugees, and internally displaced persons, to return to their places of permanent residence.

The two presidents also touched upon a number of other matters.

Tour Eiffel (1889, 324 m, looking north-west): Tour Eiffel shadow (right), Pont d'Iéna over La Seine (center down), Jardin du Trocadéro (center), Chaillot Palace (middle), tall buildings in Courbevoie near La Seine (up center, 4.5 km away).

Reports: France takes on cellphone addiction with a ban in schools.

Belgium (Population 11.4 M, rank 80, growth 0.6%. Free: 95 of 100)

European Commission, European Union, EU: 28 EU countries: Austria, Belgium, Bulgaria, Croatia, Republic of Cyprus, Czech Republic, Denmark, Estonia, Finland, France, Germany, Greece, Hungary, Ireland, Italy, Latvia, Lithuania, Luxembourg, Malta, Netherlands, Poland, Portugal, Romania, Slovakia, Slovenia, Spain, Sweden and the UK.

Germany: (Population 82.1 M, rank 16, growth 0.2%. Free: 95 of 100). Reports: Germany extends over an area of around 357,000 km^2 and has 16 federal states. Germany's three largest cities are Berlin, Hamburg and Munich. The "Oktoberfest" takes place in Munich, the "Cannstatter Wasen" in Stuttgart, and the "Freimarkt" belongs to Bremen.

19 August 2018. Talks between Vladimir Putin and Federal Chancellor of Germany Angela Merkel were held at the Meseberg residence. Prior to the talks, Vladimir Putin and Federal Chancellor of Germany Angela Merkel made press statements.

On his way to Germany, the Russian President made a private visit to Austria to attend the wedding of the republic's Foreign Minister Karin Kneissl and Wolfgang Meilinger.

20 August 2018. Reports: "Together with German partners we are working on the new natural gas pipeline Nord Stream 2, which will complete the European gas transport system," Vladimir Putin declared as he met with Chancellor Angela Merkel near Berlin on Saturday, 18 August. The project is being developed by Gazprom, along with Royal Dutch Shell, Wintershall, Uniper, OMV and Engie.

Reports: Germany's current account surplus will remain the world's largest for the third year running in 2018, at $299 B, followed by Japan with $200 B, according to the Ifo institute. "On the other end of the spectrum, the U.S. are set to remain the country with the largest current account deficit, with roughly $420 B."

Reports: The number of foreign students and researchers in Germany has been increasing for years, especially in the so-called MINT-subjects of mathematics, computer sciences, science and technology. Nearly every tenth student comes from abroad. Many are attracted to Germany by the fact that there is no tuition, others feel they will have promising prospects on the German labor market, or appreciate the high quality of teaching in Germany. According to the 2018 The World University Rankings, ten German universities are among the top 100 worldwide.

22 August 2018. Reports: "Germany is calling for the formation of a new payments system independent of the U.S., as well as creating a European Monetary Fund, and building up an independent SWIFT system, as a means of rescuing the Iranian nuclear deal. "It's essential that we strengthen European autonomy," wrote Foreign Minister Heiko Maas in Handelsblatt, stating Europe should not allow the U.S. to act "over our heads, and at our expense."

Norway (Population 5.3 M, rank 118, growth 1%. Free: 100 of 100).

Sweden (Population 9.9 M, rank 89, growth 0.7%. Free: 100 of 100). Reports: GE healthcare to open life sciences innovation center in Sweden.

Reports: Swedish biotech breaks barrier to diagnosis with rheumatoid arthritis test.

The Netherlands (Population 17 M, rank 67, growth 0.3%. Free: 99 of 100).

Czech Republic (Population 10.6 M, rank 87, growth 0.1%. Free: 94 of 100).

Denmark (Population 5.7 M, rank 114, growth 0.4%. Free: 97 of 100).

Luxembourg (Population 583 K, rank 169, growth 1.3%. Free: 98 of 100).

Spain: (Population 46.3 M, rank 30, growth 0%. Free: 94 of 100).

Portugal: (Population 10.3 M, rank 88, decrease 0.4%. Free: 97 of 100).

India, Pakistan, Australia, and neighbors

India (Population: 1.3 B, rank 2nd, growth 1.1%. Free: 77 of 100). 17 August 2018. The President of Russia sent a message of condolences to President of India, Ram Nath Kovind, and Prime Minister of India, Narendra Modi, on the passing of Atal Bihari Vajpayee, outstanding statesman and former prime minister of India.

20 August 2018. The President of Russia sent a message to the President of India Ram Nath Kovind, and Prime Minister of India Narendra Modi, expressing condolences over the loss of life caused by devastating floods in the state of Kerala.

Reports: India's health ministry is calling for stopping the sale or import of electronic cigarettes, and heat-not-burn tobacco devices that companies like Philip Morris were planning to launch in the country. The country has 106 M adult smokers, second only to China. In recent years, the government has intensified its tobacco-control efforts, raising cigarette taxes, and ordering companies to print bigger health warnings.

30 August 2018. Reports: In response to the fall of Argentina's peso, other fragile emerging market currencies sold off sharply overnight, with Turkey's lira and the South African rand feeling heat, and India's rupee slumping to a new record low. The tumult highlights a heavy international dependence on the dollar. Some 48% of the world's $30 T in cross-border loans are priced in the U.S. currency, up from 40% a decade ago.

Indonesia: (Population: 263.9 M, rank 4, growth 1.1%. Partly free: 65 of 100). 25 August 2018. The President of Russia sent his condolences to Indonesia's President, Joko Vidodo, over the numerous casualties and major destruction caused by a strong earthquake on the island of Lombok.

Australia: (Population: 24.4 M, rank 53, growth 1.3%. Free: 98 of 100). 20 August 2018. Reports: Australian Prime Minister Malcolm Turnbull has survived a leadership challenge, after struggling to pass key pieces of his legislative agenda, and keep members of his party in line. A bid to cut corporate taxes has stalled in Parliament, a devastating drought is threatening to hurt growth, and an argument with China over political interference has chilled relations with the country's top trading partner.

23 August 2018. Reports: Australian Prime Minister Malcolm Turnbull is fighting to stay in power, despite senior ministers deserting him, saying he would only hold a second leadership vote on Friday, 24 August, if he received a letter signed by the majority of the ruling party. Former home affairs minister Peter Dutton has declared he would again contest a Liberal party leadership vote, while reports suggest the country's treasurer and foreign minister may also be candidates.

23 August 2018. Reports: Souring relations between China and Australia have seen Huawei and ZTE banned from providing 5G technology equipment in Australia. "The government considers that the involvement of vendors who are likely to be subject to extrajudicial directions from a foreign government that conflict with Australian law, may risk failure by the carrier to adequately protect a 5G network from unauthorized access or interference," according to a statement from Australia's Department of Communications.

24 August 2018. Reports: Australia is set for its sixth prime minister in the past decade, after Treasurer Scott Morrison prevailed in a leadership ballot to replace Malcolm Turnbull, whose position got shakier over the past week. With his party moving further to the right, Morrison is considered a conservative choice.

27 August 2018. Reports: Australia's new Prime Minister Scott Morrison is shaking up his cabinet with a new foreign minister, as well as a host of other positions, in a bid to heal divisions following a week of political chaos. An opinion poll published by The Australian newspaper on Sunday showed Labor leading the government by 56% to 44% on a two party preferred basis - the worst figures in a decade for the Liberal-National coalition.

New Zealand: (Population 4.7 M, rank 125, growth 1%. Free: 98 of 100).

Pakistan: (Population 212 M, rank 5, growth 2%. Partly free: 43 of 100). Reports about Pakistan's future under Imran Khan. Many challenges are expected, and all these challenges will be compounded by Khan's inexperience — he's never held national power — and by a polarized political environment, featuring a very unhappy opposition.

4 September 2018. Reports: The Pentagon has made a final decision to cancel $300 M in aid to Pakistan that had been suspended over Islamabad's perceived failure to take decisive action against militants. Another $500 M in Coalition Support Funds was stripped by Congress earlier this year, piling further pressure on the struggling Pakistani economy. Forex reserves have plummeted this year as the nation debates whether to seek a bailout from the IMF or friendly nations like China.

Philippines: (Population 104.9 M, rank 13, growth 1.5%. Partly free 63 of 100).

Singapore: (Population 5.7 M, rank 115, growth 1.5%. Partly free 51 of 100). 6 August 2018. Reports: At a regional forum in Singapore, the Asian economic bloc vowed to double down on trade pacts to minimize economic damage in the region, which is particularly exposed to fallout from the U.S.-China trade battle. Singapore's foreign minister also urged the 10 ASEAN nations (Indonesia, Thailand, Singapore, Malaysia, Vietnam, Philippines, Myanmar (Burma), Cambodia, Laos, Brunei) to quickly conclude talks for a Comprehensive Economic Partnership trade agreement that includes China and Japan, but not the U.S.

Thailand: (Population 69 M, rank 20, growth 0.3%. Not free 32 of 100).

Myanmar (Burma, Population 53.3 M, rank 26, growth 0.9%. Not free 32 of 100

Bangladesh (Population 164.6 M, rank 8, growth 1.1%. Partly free 47 of 100). Reports: Bangladesh is not in the news, but, given recent developments over there, the country appears to be a powder barrel, and it could explode.

Sri Lanka (Population 20.8 M, rank 58, growth 0.4%. Partly free 56 of 100).

Malaysia (Population 31.6 M, rank 45, growth 1.34%. Partly free 44 of 100).

Brunei: (Population 428,000, rank 176, growth 1.3%. Not free 29 of 100).

Vanuatu: (Population 276,000, rank 185, growth 2.2%. Free 80 of 100)

Mausoleum (135-139) of Hadrian (76–138, Emperor 117-138, renamed Castel Sant'Angelo in 600), on Via Lungotevere Castelo.

Italy, Middle East, Africa

Italy: (Population 59.3 M, rank 23, decrease 0.1%. Free: 89 of 100). 8 August 2018. Reports: While reiterating his commitment to a prudent fiscal policy, Italy's economy minister has lowered upcoming GDP growth estimates, bringing the deficit to 1.2% in 2019 (higher than a target of 0.8% drawn up by the previous administration). The worsening expectations could put the new anti-establishment government on a collision course with the European Commission, which monitors the budgets of EU countries.

14 August 2018. The President of Russia sent a message of sincere condolences to President of Italy, Sergio Mattarella, over the tragic consequences of a bridge collapse near the city of Genoa.

20 August 2018. Reports: Renewed market tremors last week over Italian debt, and attacks by politicians in Rome on Europe's establishment, are fueling fresh fears that all is not well with the euro.

An Italian biotech company makes wood-derived bone implants.

Vatican: (Population 792, rank 233 (last), decrease 1.1%).

San Marino: (Population 33,400, rank 218, growth 0.6%. Free 97 of 100)

Jordan (Population 9.7 M, rank 92, growth 2.6%. Partly free, 37 of 100). 21 August 2018. The President of Russia had a telephone conversation with King Abdullah II of the Hashemite Kingdom of Jordan. The leaders exchanged greetings on the 55th anniversary of diplomatic relations between the two states, and expressed their satisfaction with the friendly and constructive nature of Russian-Jordanian cooperation. The discussion covered various aspects of the settlement process in Syria. In this context, they noted the effective cooperation between the two countries' corresponding ministries and agencies. Special attention was paid to the work done to return Syrian refugees and displaced persons.

Lebanon: (Population: 6 M, rank 111, growth 1.3%. Partly free: 44 of 100). Reports: The numbers of migrant domestic workers in Lebanon, as well as the gulf states, are rising dramatically, but the conditions for them remain well substandard.

United Arab Emirates (UAE) (Population: 9.4 M, rank 94, growth 1.4%. Not free, 20 of 100).

Saudi Arabia (Population 32.9 M, rank 41, growth 2.1%. Not free: 10 of 100). 6 August 2018. Reports: Saudi Arabia is severing all new business and investment transactions with Canada after the government in Ottawa expressed concern over recent arrests of civil society and women's rights activists in the kingdom. It also gave the Canadian ambassador 24 hours to leave the country and recalled its own ambassador to Canada, saying it retained "its rights to take further action."

8 August 2018. Reports: Saudi Arabia has stopped all medical treatment programs in Canada, and is coordinating for the transfer of all Saudi patients from Canadian hospitals to facilities outside the country. Riyadh froze new trade and investment with the North American nation, and expelled the Canadian ambassador on Monday, in a stern gesture of retaliation after Ottawa urged it to free arrested civil society activists.

Yemen (Population 28.2 M, rank 50, growth 2.4%. Not free: 14 of 100).

Iraq (Population 38.2 M, rank 36, growth 2.9%. Not free: 27 of 100). 10 August 2018. Reports: The alliance of populist Shiite cleric Moqtada al-Sadr won Iraq's legislative election in May, according to a manual recount, paving the way for a coalition to be formed nearly three months after the polls. The next government faces a daunting list of challenges: reforming the economy, fighting corruption, rebuilding areas destroyed in the war against Islamic State, and preventing a resurgence of the terrorist group.

21 August 2018. Reports: Iraq's economy is so closely linked to Iran that Baghdad is going to ask Washington for permission to

ignore some U.S. sanctions on its neighbor, according to government and central bank officials. The request would mark an important change in political tactics for Iraqi Prime Minister Haider al-Abadi. He initially said Baghdad would respect all the U.S. sanctions, but faced heavy criticism from rivals.

Iran: (Population 81.1 M, rank 18, growth 1.1%. Not free: 17 of 100. 9 August 2018. Reports: Iranian President Hassan Rouhani told North Korea's foreign minister that the Americans cannot be trusted, adding that Tehran and Pyongyang have "always had close views" on many issues. Supreme Leader Ayatollah Ali Khamenei also said the Islamic Republic had nothing to be concerned about "at all," and that "nobody can do anything."

12 August 2018. Reports: President of Russia met with President of the Islamic Republic of Iran, Hassan Rouhani, on the sidelines of the Caspian Summit. The two presidents addressed ways in which they can settle the world's most acute crises, particularly in the Middle East. President of Russia Vladimir Putin: Mr. President, I am very glad to have the opportunity to personally meet with you on the sidelines of the summit and exchange opinions on a whole range of various issues.

There is much cooperation between our countries. We have many issues to address regarding the world's acute crises, including that in Syria. I would like to inform you about the progress of our contacts with our partners on this complicated problem.

Although our colleagues are in constant contact with each other, personal meetings at such level are highly important.

President of Iran Hassan Rouhani: Mr. President,

I am very glad to have this opportunity to meet with you on the sidelines of the Caspian Summit. And I am very glad that with each year our relations are developing positively.

Recently, Iran has officially reinforced its cooperation with the Eurasian Economic Union. This may make for the development of trade between our countries.

Another sphere of our interaction is bilateral cooperation in fighting terrorism and bringing stability to the region.

Our common goal is to establish stability and peace in the whole region and provide security for the region's countries. The world has witnessed how, with the help from Iran and Russia, the Syrian army was able to play a vital role in fighting terrorism in Syria.

I must emphasize that today all measures being taken by Iran, Russia and Turkey are helping to establish peace and security in the Syrian Arab Republic. In the recent years, we have reached two important achievements. The first one is cooperation between Iran, Russia and other countries in achieving agreements on the Iranian Nuclear Deal. The second one is how Iran, Russia and Turkey cooperate in establishing peace and security in Syria. We are committed to the elimination of any hurdles and the settling of any global crises solely within the framework of dialogue and talks.

20 August 2018. Reports: Iran said it will unveil a new fighter jet when it celebrates National Defense Industry Day on Aug. 22, and will continue developing missile capabilities. The Islamic Republic's navy also announced that it mounted a locally built advanced defensive weapons system on one of its warships for the first time, as tensions rise in the Persian Gulf.

28 August 2018. Reports: It's the first time Iran's parliament summoned President Hassan Rouhani, who is under pressure from hardline rivals to change his cabinet after growing economic difficulties. "The problems are critical, but more important than that is that many people have lost their faith in the future of the Islamic Republic, and are in doubt about its power," he said. "We will overcome the troubles."

Israel: (Population 8.3 M, rank 100, growth 1.6%. Free: 80 of 100).

Palestine: (Population 4.9 M (rank 121, grows 2.7%). Not free: 28 of 100).

Egypt (Population 97.5 M (rank 14, grows 1.9%). Not free, 26 of 100).

League of Arab States (LAS) (22 countries: Algeria, Bahrein, Comoros, Djibouti, Egypt, Iraq, Jordan, Kuwait, Lebanon, Libya, Mauritania, Morocco, Oman, Palestine, Qatar, Saudi Arabia, Somalia, Sudan, Syria, Tunisia, United Arab Emirates and Yemen).

Qatar: (Population 2.6 M (rank 142, grows 2.7%). Not free: 26 of 100). 4 September 2018. Reports: Qatar plans to invest billions of dollars more in Germany, and will broaden its focus to the country's medium-sized companies, according to Handelsblatt. As the world's biggest exporter of liquefied natural gas, Qatar has shareholdings in companies including Volkswagen, Deutsche Bank, Siemens, Hochtief, and SolarWorld, which reportedly amount to $20 B.

Kuwait: (Population 4.1 M (rank 130, grows 2.1%). Partly free: 36 of 100).

Oman: (Population 4.6 M (rank 127, grows 4.8%). Not free: 25 of 100)

Bahrain: (Population 1.5 M (rank 152, grows 4.7%). Not free: 12 of 100). Reports: MANAMA, Bahrain -- Bahraini carrier Gulf Air is looking to reduce fuel costs by streamlining operations across its Airbus and Boeing fleet with Honeywell's GoDirect Flight Efficiency software.

Syria: (Population 18.2 M (rank 63, decrease 0.9%). Not free: 0 of 100).

Kenya: (Population 49.7 M (rank 28, growth 2.6%. Partly free, 51 of 100).

Libya: (Population 6.3 M, rank 109, growth 1.3%. Not free: 13 of 100).

Tunisia: (Population 11.5 M, rank 78, growth 1.1%. Free: 78 of 100).

Morocco: (Population 35.7 M, rank 39, growth 1.3%. Partly free: 41 of 100).

South Africa: (Population 56.7 M, rank 25, growth 1.3%. Free, 78 of 100). 23 August 2018. Reports: President Trump raised concerns about Pretoria's land reform plans. He instructed Secretary of State Mike Pompeo to look at the changes proposed by the ruling ANC, as well as the "expropriations and large-scale killing of farmers." Many are already concerned about the country's weak economic growth, ballooning public debt, and policy missteps.

Zimbabwe: (Population 16.5 M, rank 70, growth 2.4%. Partly Free, 32 of 100).

Sudan (Population 40.5 M, rank 35, growth 2.4%. Not Free: 6 of 100).

South Sudan (Population 12.5 M, rank 76, growth 2.8%. Not Free: 4 of 100)

Guinea: (Population 12.7 M, rank 75, growth 2.6%. Partly Free, 41 of 100).

Djibouti (Population 957,000, rank 160, growth 1.6%. Not Free: 26 of 100).

Somalia: (Population 14.7 M, rank 74, growth 3%. Not free: 5 of 100).

Niger (Population 21.4 M, rank 57, growth 3.9%. Partly free: 49 of 100).

Nigeria (Population 190.8 M, rank 7, growth 2.6%. Partly free: 50 of 100).

Cameroon (Population 24 M, rank 55, growth 2.6%. Not free: 24 of 100).

Sierra Leone: (Population 7.5 M (rank 103, grows 2.2%). Partly free: 66 of 100)

Chad: (Population 15 M (rank 73, grows 3.1%). Not free: 18 of 100).

The Gambia: (Population 2.1 M (rank 146, grows 3%). Not free: 20 of 100).

Malawi: (Population 18.6 M (rank 61, grows 2.9%). Partly free: 63 of 100).

Rwanda: (Population 12.2 M (rank 77, grows 2.4%). Not free: 24 of 100).

Burkina Faso: (Population 19.1 M (rank 60, grows 2.9%). Partly free: 63 of 100).

Central African Republic: (Population 4.6 M (rank 126, grows 1.4%). Not free: 10 of 100).

Senegal: (Population 15.8 M (rank 72, grows 2.8%). Free: 78 of 100).

Gabon: (Population 2 M (rank 149, grows 2.3%). Partly Free: 32 of 100).

Madagascar: (Population 25.5 M (rank 51, grows 2.7%). Partly Free: 56 of 100).

Democratic Republic of the Congo: (Population 81.3 M (rank 17, grows 3.3%). Not Free: 19 of 100). 6 August 2018. Reports: Vaccinations against a new Ebola outbreak in eastern Democratic Republic of the Congo, believed to have killed 33 people, are due to begin on Wednesday, 8 August. The experimental vaccine, which is manufactured by Merck, proved successful during its first wide-scale usage against an outbreak in northwestern Congo, that was declared over less than two weeks ago. More than 3,000 doses remain in stock in the capital, Kinshasa.

22 August 2018. Reports: Democratic Republic of Congo has approved four more experimental treatments against the deadly Ebola virus, as the country races to contain a new outbreak. They include Remdesivir, made by Gilead Sciences; ZMapp, an intravenous treatment made by San Diego's Mapp Pharmaceutical; Japanese drug Favipiravir; and one referred to as Regn3450 - 3471 - 3479. In addition, a vaccine manufactured by Merck has been administered to 1,693 health workers and contacts of Ebola patients.

Angola: (Population 29.7 M (rank 46, grows 3.4%). Not Free: 24 of 100).

Zambia: (Population 17 M (rank 66, grows 3%). Partly Free: 56 of 100).

Boston Harbor (1614): Rowes Wharf (1666, 1764, 1987): the stern (rear) of Clipper Stad Amsterdam (2000, 76 m x 10.5 m x 4.8 m x 46.5 m) moored here, with the poop deck clearly visible.

Medical

MoCA is a routine screening test for cognitive impairment in older adults, that's widely used by doctors in the United States. Although MoCA isn't intended to prove or disprove definitively whether someone is experiencing problems with thinking or memory, it can be a helpful tool when used as part of an overall assessment by doctors trained to diagnose cognitive problems.

Engineers and medical researchers at the University of Minnesota have teamed up to create a groundbreaking added manufacturing device that could someday help patients, with long-term spinal cord injuries, regain some function.
– University of Minnesota College of Science and Engineering Advanced Functional Materials

A new systematic review provides the most comprehensive assessment to date on the scientific evidence estimating the effectiveness of various fertility awareness-based methods (FABMs) for contraception. – University of North Carolina Health Care System, Obstetrics & Gynecology

About 1 million Americans go to the hospital with pneumonia every year. Pneumonia is a lung infection caused by pneumococcal disease, which can also cause blood infections and meningitis.

Researchers created the first 3D placenta model, which helps study pregnancy disorders.

Seaweed-derived treatment for common cold was approved in the EU.

Depression is unusually common among people with Alzheimer's disease. In the general population, about 6% of men and women over 65 have a bout of the blues each year. By contrast, 40 to 50% of people with Alzheimer's experience some symptoms of depression. And 10 to 20% develop a longer-lasting, more severe form of the mood disorder, known as major, or clinical, depression. Moreover, depression rates are elevated among people who have other types of dementia, as well as among individuals with mild cognitive impairment (MCI), a condition that often precedes Alzheimer's.

Doctors have also observed that some people with Alzheimer's and other forms of dementia experience symptoms not normally associated with depression. Perhaps the first clear portrait of this situation comes from a 2003 study in *The American Journal of Psychiatry*. Researchers assessed 394 elderly people to determine if they suffered from depression; 243 were presumed to have Alzheimer's and 151 were cognitively healthy. Nearly 50 percent of people with Alzheimer's had experienced at least one episode of major depression during their lifetimes, as had 28 percent of their cognitively healthy counterparts.

A valuable cache of brain cancer biomedical data, one of only two such large collections in the country, has been made freely available worldwide by researchers at Georgetown Lombardi Comprehensive Cancer Center. Nature

Each year, about 1 million prostate biopsies are performed in the United States, and of those, about one in three are cancerous.

New study by researchers at Intermountain Medical Center in Salt Lake City found that patients with low-risk blood clots may be better off receiving treatment at home, versus being admitted to the hospital. - CHEST, Aug 2018

Mount Sinai researchers discover how to restore vision using retinal stem cells. Study could lead to cures for blinding diseases. – Mount Sinai Health System, Nature

Researchers at the University of California San Diego School of Medicine report that women whose mothers lived to at least age 90 were more likely to also live to 90, free of serious diseases and disabilities. – University of California San Diego Health, Age and Aging

A first-of-its-kind global study shows that children in 27 developing countries have better nutrition — when they live near forests. – University of Vermont, Science Advances, August 15

When physicians follow computer alerts embedded in electronic health records, their hospitalized patients experience fewer complications and lower costs, leave the hospital sooner and are less likely to be readmitted, according to a study of inpatients. – Cedars-Sinai, The American Journal of Managed Care

Muscles of the elderly and of patients with Duchene muscular dystrophy have trouble regenerating. A new nanohydrogel with muscle stem cells has boosted muscle growth in mouse models, while protecting the stem cells from immune reactions that usually appear. – Georgia Institute of Technology
Science Advances, August 2018

Pedestrian injuries and fatalities in the U.S. have steadily increased during recent years. In 2015, 5,376 pedestrians were killed and 70,000 injured. Prior research showed an association between the number of neighborhood alcohol stores and risk of pedestrian injuries. – Research Society on Alcoholism
Alcoholism: Clinical and Experimental Research

Research shows that more seniors could live longer, despite cognitive decline. – University of Kentucky

The food-borne illness outbreak, that sickened hundreds of Chipotle Mexican Grill customers in Ohio last month, was caused by a type of bacteria found in meat and pre-cooked food left at unsafe temperatures, according to the Centers for Disease Control and Prevention. The outbreak was the latest in a series of food safety lapses at Chipotle, and the CDC says it was caused by the clostridium perfringens bacterium, which often infects food that is prepared in large quantities and left out - not cold enough and not hot enough - for several hours after being cooked.

New research from Massachusetts Eye and Ear and MIT suggests that glaucoma may be an autoimmune disease. This finding reveals a promising new therapeutic target for this blinding condition, and sheds light on a disease-causing process in glaucoma that has largely remained a mystery, until now.

The second leading cause of blindness worldwide, glaucoma is a group of eye conditions that often cause irreparable damage to the optic nerve, which transmits visual information from the eye to the brain. Elevated eye pressure is a hallmark of glaucoma, but it has not been well understood how or why this pressure leads to permanent vision loss. Furthermore, not all patients with elevated eye pressure go on to develop glaucoma, and some patients still lose their vision even after their eye pressure has been treated.

In a study led by co-senior author Dong Feng Chen, MD, PhD, a vision scientist at Mass. Eye and Ear, and associate professor of ophthalmology at Harvard Medical School, the researchers found that when pressure in the eye rises, it induces the expression of a family of proteins that develop in response to stressful conditions. This then triggers a response from immune cells called memory T cells, which attack the nerve cells of the retina, leading to optic nerve damage and often permanent vision loss. Importantly, the researchers observed this immune response in both mouse models of glaucoma, and blood samples of patients with primary open angle glaucoma (POAG). These findings, published online in the journal *Nature Communications*, open the door to targeting T cells in the eye to halt the progression of vision loss in glaucoma, potentially providing a new sight-saving therapy for patients.

Maple trees are best known for their maple syrup and lovely fall foliage. But it turns out that the beauty of those leaves could be skin-deep — and that's a good thing. Today, scientists report that an extract from the leaves may prevent wrinkles. – 256th National Meeting & Exposition of the American Chemical Society (ACS)

Scientists report they have successfully developed and tested the world's first ultrathin artificial retina that could vastly improve on existing implantable visualization technology for the blind. The flexible device, based on very thin 2D materials. – 256th National Meeting & Exposition of the American Chemical Society (ACS)

58   Dediu Newsletter Vol 2, Number 10 (22), 6 September 2018

Inflammatory bowel disease (IBD) is a set of painful conditions that can cause severe diarrhea and fatigue. Treatments can include medications and surgery. But now researchers report that a simple dietary intervention with strawberries could mitigate colonic inflammation. – 256th National Meeting & Exposition of the American Chemical Society (ACS).

Diacomit was approved for treatment of dravet syndrome seizures.

HDL cholesterol may be known as the "good" kind, but a new study suggests high levels of it are not always a good thing for women after menopause.

FDA approves first drug for rare neurotrophic keratitis eye disease.

Researchers create more than a dozen drugs to curb smoking.

Biological engineers discover new antibiotic candidates.

Probiotics are in yogurt, pickles, and bread.

Insomnia is the most common sleep disorder in the U.S., affecting nearly one out of every three adults at some point in life. More women suffer from insomnia than men, and as people get older, insomnia becomes more prevalent.
Most experts agree that adults need seven to nine hours of sleep a night. According to the National Sleep Foundation, the average American only gets about 6.9 hours.

In France there is a new domain of research regarding the connection between cancer and obesity – in French: Metabo-Oncologie: Au croisement du Cancer et de l'Obésité – Un domaine émergent de la recherche et du traitement du cancer.

FDA approved Imbruvica plus Rituximab for rare blood cancer.

Aspirin disappoints for avoiding first heart attack, or stroke.

Blood pressure and cholesterol drugs continue to improve survival.

A study led by Columbia University cardiologist Mathew Maurer showed that tafamidis reduces deaths and hospitalizations from an underdiagnosed type of heart failure called transthyretin amyloid cardiomyopathy. The drug could be one of the first effective treatments for the disease.
– Columbia University Irving Medical Center

It appears that diet has bigger impact on emotional well-being in women than in men. Women may need a more nutrient-rich diet to support a positive emotional well-being, according to new research from Binghamton University, State University at New York.

FDA issues more warnings to online networks selling illegal opioids.

Pfizer issues voluntary nationwide recall of one lot of children's Advil.

Labeling mix-up: Accord Healthcare issues voluntary recall of hydrochlorothiazide tablets.

Cycle Pharmaceuticals receives FDA approval for Ketorolac Tromethamine tablets.

A person with osteoporosis typically has low bone density, poor bone quality, and fragile bones. Some people think the condition occurs only in women, but older men are at risk, too. Because men with prostate cancer tend to be older, they are at risk for age-related declines in bone density. Moreover, men undergoing androgen-deprivation therapy for CRPC are at increased risk for loss of bone density, due to treatment side effects. Research suggests that men can lose 2 to 6% of their bone mineral density in the first year

of androgen-deprivation therapy. Loss of bone continues in the second year but at a much slower rate. Bone health is also compromised by cancer that has spread to the bone.
Bone loss can result in such skeletal-related events as painful fractures and falls, loss of ability and independence, and a reduced quality of life. To detect osteoporosis early, it is recommended that men with advanced prostate cancer undergo regular bone-density screening with dual-energy X-ray absorptiometry (DXA) scanning. This technique is the gold standard for measuring bone mineral density. It is a simple, painless test that takes approximately 20 minutes, and exposure to radiation is low. Further, it is recommended that clinicians caring for patients with CRPC offer preventive treatment with supplemental calcium and vitamin D.

Hearing loss and dizziness are two of the most common reasons why people visit their doctors, especially as they age. The main ear-related problems are tinnitus, imbalance and vertigo.

Tiny protein structures, called amyloids, are key to understanding certain devastating age-related diseases. Aggregates, or sticky clumped-up amyloids, form plaques in the brain, and are the main culprits in the progression of Alzheimer's and Huntington's diseases. – Washington University in St. Louis ChemBioChem

Researchers at the University of Florida have discovered that a modified version of an important immune cell protein could be used to treat Alzheimer's disease. – The Rockefeller University Press, Journal of Experimental Medicine, September 2018

Researchers observed medical vision problems and other ills related to playing videogames.

Many people, who regularly take the pain reliever ibuprofen, unknowingly exceed the daily dosing limits, according to a study in *Pharmacoepidemiology & Drug Safety*. Ibuprofen is a nonsteroidal anti-inflammatory drug (NSAID). And NSAIDs, especially when taken long term or overused, have a range of potential adverse effects, including gastrointestinal bleeding, increased risk of heart attacks and strokes, and kidney damage.

Swift gene-editing method may revolutionize treatments for cancer and infectious diseases.

Mathematics, Science & Artificial Intelligence (AI)

Intel sold $1 B of artificial intelligence processor chips in 2017, the first time the world's second-largest chipmaker disclosed revenue from the fast-growing computing segment. As PC sales stagnate, Intel has increasingly been depending on its sales to data centers, which provide computing power for mobile and web-based apps. Those programs, in turn, rely on AI for features like photo and speech recognition.

Boeing and its subsidiary Aurora Flight Sciences are hoping to advance the design and construction of autonomous aircraft, and associated technologies, through the establishment of a new center for autonomous flying vehicle R&D at MIT's Kendall Square, in Cambridge, Massachusetts.

Historic space weather (due to the Sun) may help us understand what's coming next, according to new research by the University of Warwick. Space Weather

Earlier this year, Google began testing Bristlecone, a quantum computer chip that its creators think will soon achieve "quantum supremacy," the point when it can outperform the world's fastest supercomputers.

Understanding of protons and neutrons, or "nucleons" — the building blocks of atomic nuclei — has advanced dramatically, both theoretically and experimentally, in the past half century, with the help of electron-ion collider.

Bioenergy with carbon capture and storage (BECCS) is a technology that integrates biomass conversion to heat, electricity, or liquid or gas fuels, with carbon capture and sequestration. BECCS could provide a significant portion of the global energy supply, if deployed to its theoretical maximum feasible amount.

New technologies and approaches are generating large, diverse data sets, and data science offers the tools that are needed to interrogate, analyze, and manage these data sets.

Integration of Simulation Science and Data Science has been a key topic of discussion about the future of cyberinfrastructure for science and engineering research.

On August 23, 2018, the National Academies of Sciences, Engineering and Medicine will conduct a colloquium to explore some of the latest developments in quantum sensing and quantum communications.

Manufacturers have been known to label containers with statements such as, "Product sold by weight, not by volume" or "Contents may settle during shipping and handling." Consumers may also be advised to mix the powder, or to shake the container for best results before using. To improve product uniformity, and improve consumer perception related to fill volume in container, specialists work on new ways to minimize changes in bulk density of powders, from time of manufacture until consumer use.

Machine learning and artificial intelligence (AI) are having a dramatic impact on the medical device field. The current development and application for diagnostic and therapeutic applications, like precision-targeted AI in medical devices, are expected to grow fast once true artificial intelligence is implemented.

Computer scientists work to build robots who get the joke. Appreciating humor may be vital for future co-operation between humans and machines.

Researchers are working on new and on proven technologies for a cost-efficient storage of hydrogen, that allows for the transport between different locations, and the management of hydrogen as a useful industrial resource in their operations and plants.

Biological fouling, or biofouling, is the accumulation of waterborne organisms on submerged surfaces. This buildup on ships not only slows down the passage of these vessels through the water, but it can also serve as a route for the transfer of invasive aquatic species into an ecosystem. Therefore, the specialists are working on a new method to treat biofouling on ships while in port.

There is need for innovative services and products, for industrial and commercial customers worldwide, that leverage collected energy-related data, as well as data from other sources.

Mathematicians are working on an algorithm that can rapidly, accurately, and automatically colorize grey scale panchromatic images.

Producing biofuel with seawater could be cost-effective and eco-friendly.

The Industrial Synthetic Biology Congress on 8-9 October in Munich comes at a time when synthetic biology is important in biomanufacturing. Areas of interest are:
Genetic and Computational Tool Development
Synthetic Biology for Industrial Chemical Production
Synthetic Biology Platforms for Natural Products, Drug Discovery and Development
Synthetic Biology Biofuels

A team of researchers from Penn State's Materials Research Institute, and the University of Utah, has developed a wearable energy harvesting device that could generate energy from low-frequency vibrations, like the swing of an arm while walking or jogging. – Advanced Functional Materials, Aug-2018

Robotics is reshaping people's lives through its entry into our homes, and by its performance of medical procedures and therapeutic applications. To allow robotics to gain further access into human lives, designers will have to apply a human-centric approach, recreating robotic designs that are less metal and mechanical, and more human-like. As robots become more affordable and accessible, they are showing up in a wide variety of applications, from medicine to farming to scientific exploration and textile assembly lines—some of which is very delicate work. Humanizing robots, by providing them with a more natural, human-like form and social presence, is a difficult challenge. This humanization requires an intersection of integrative biosciences, material science, mechanics and electronics, to make robots behave and look more like everyday people.

New mathematical models developed by the Department of Energy's Oak Ridge National Laboratory, with collaborators at Sam Houston State University and the University of Chicago, can help guide changes to the layout of poor urban unstructured neighborhoods. – Science Advances, Aug-2018.

Fillers are additives that increase the bulk weight of a food product. This allows food to be produced inexpensively; however, fillers are generally low in nutritional value. With the movement toward consuming whole foods from natural sources, the specialists are working on an alternative material to replace maltodextrin and corn syrup solids in food products.

Scientists have released the most accurate, high-resolution terrain map of Antarctica ever created. The new map has a resolution of 2 to 8 meters, compared to 1,000 meters, which was typical for previous maps. – Ohio State University

Elon Musk and Jeff Bezos both have big dreams in outer space — sending man into orbit, onto Moon and Mars. Musk has SpaceX, Bezos has Blue Origins.

General news and issues

19 August – World Photography Day.

The fragrances business is $40 B/year.

Global dividends jumped 12.9% year-on-year in Q2 to $497.4 B, hitting a new record, according to a report on the Janus Henderson Global Dividend Index. Payments rose in almost every region of the world in headline terms, and records were broken in 12 countries including France, Japan, and the U.S. The index also ended the quarter at a fresh high of 182.0, meaning that global dividends have risen by more than four-fifths since 2009.

A new research shows that entertainment media shape people's beliefs in ways they aren't aware of.

Reports about the non-validity of many experiments: researchers cannot replicate about half of the social studies experiments published in top journals.

Humor

A young wife tells her husband:
- Over 2400 years ago, Sophocles said: "Without labor nothing prospers".
What would he say now?
The husband very serious:
- "With politicians nothing prospers!"

The husband, his wife and their 6 years boy go to shop. Sure enough, the boy gets bored, and asks mommy:
- When do we go home?
- In a couple of minutes, responds mommy with a smile.
- A couple of minutes? - asks the boy a little confused.
The father intervenes to help:
- 5, 10, 15 minutes….

The whole family comes to the grandpa:
- Happy Birthday Grandpa!
- My birthday? – responds grandpa surprised.
- Yes, grandpa, your 85th birthday! - the whole family confirms.
The grandpa is even more surprised:
- But I never was so old!?

Universe Axioms

Formulated by Michael M. Dediu

The following axioms are not independent of each other. They express in different ways the same concept of infinity.

Axiom 1. Pointing a theoretical laser from Earth, in any direction, at any time, after a finite amount of time the laser beam will touch an astronomic body.

Axiom 2. In any direction in space starting from Earth, at any time, there is an astronomic body from which the Earth can be theoretically seen.

Axiom 3. Infinity of space: Any straight line passing through the Earth's center intersects an infinite number of astronomic bodies.

Axiom 4. Infinity of time: Representing the time on a line, with the origin at the beginning of the year 1, the time goes to infinite in both positive and negative directions.

Axiom 5. Infinity of life: Because of the infinity of space and time, it is normal to consider that the life exists at any time, in an infinite number of places. Therefore right now, when you are reading this book, there is life outside the Earth, in an infinite number of places, but we do not know yet how to contact them.

Axiom 6. The Earth rotates itself around its polar axis, the Moon and many artificial satellites rotate around the Earth, in the Solar System all the planets and many other objects rotate around the Sun, the Solar System itself rotates around the center of the Milky Way galaxy, the Milky Way galaxy and all the billions of galaxies in our Universe (denoted U_1) rotate around the center of our Universe U_1, our Universe U_1, together with billions of other similar Universes, are inside a bigger Universe U_2 and rotate around the center of U_2, then U_2 and many others like it are inside a bigger U_3 and rotate around the center of U_3, and so on. Therefore, in general, the Universe U_n together with many similar Universes are inside the bigger Universe U_{n+1} and rotate around the center of U_{n+1}, for any n natural number, which goes to infinity. This can be written in the formula:

$$U_1 \subset U_2 \subset U_3 \subset \ldots \subset U_n \subset U_{n+1} \subset \ldots, \text{ n natural number.}$$

UK, Oxford, Oriel College (1326, in the east range of First quadrangle, the ornate portico in the center, with the inscription Regnante Carolo).

Time Axioms

Formulated by Michael M. Dediu

Axiom 1. Time is the most important force in the Univers.

Axiom 2. Everything is a function of time.

Axiom 3. Time exists in absolutely everything.

Axiom 4. Time creates and distroys everything.

Axiom 5. Time is invisible, inodor, insipid, unpalpabil, unaudible, but exists evrywhere.

Axiom 6. There are infinitezimal time particles, without mass, which are present everywhere, and which actually continuously transform everything.

UK, Cambridge, From Trinity Lane looking south to the west part of the northern façade and entrance of King's College Chapel (1446).

Bibliography

"The Histories" by Polybius

"Discours de la Méthode" by René Descartes

"Meditationes de prima philosophia" by René Descartes

"Philosophiae Naturalis Principia Mathematica" by Isaac Newton

Chinese encyclopedia Gujin Tushu Jicheng (Imperial Encyclopedia)

"Encyclopédie" by Jean-Baptiste le Rond d'Alembert and Denis Diderot

"Encyclopaedia Britannica" by over 4,400 contributors

"Encyclopedia Americana" by Francis Lieber

Michael M. Dediu is also the author of these books (which can be found on Amazon.com, and www.derc.com):

1. Aphorisms and quotations – with examples and explanations
2. Axioms, aphorisms and quotations – with examples and explanations
3. 100 Great Personalities and their Quotations
4. Professor Petre P. Teodorescu – A Great Mathematician and Engineer
5. Professor Ioan Goia – A Dedicated Engineering Professor
6. Venice (Venezia) – a new perspective. A short presentation with photographs
7. La Serenissima (Venice) - a new photographic perspective. A short presentation with many photos
8. Grand Canal – Venice. A new photographic viewpoint. A short presentation with many photos
9. Piazza San Marco – Venice. A different photographic view. A short presentation with many photos
10. Roma (Rome) - La Città Eterna. A new photographic view. A short presentation with many photos
11. Why is Rome so Fascinating? A short presentation with many photos
12. Rome, Boston and Helsinki. A short photographic presentation
13. Rome and Tokyo – two captivating cities. A short photographic presentation
14. Beautiful Places on Earth – A new photographic presentation

15. From Niagara Falls to Mount Fuji via Rome - A novel photographic presentation

16. From the USA and Canada to Italy and Japan - A fresh photographic presentation

17. Paris – Why So Many Call This City Mon Amour - A lovely photographic presentation

18. The City of Light – Paris (La Ville-Lumière) - A kaleidoscopic photographic presentation

19. Paris (Lutetia Parisiorum) – the romance capital of the world - A kaleidoscopic photographic view

20. Paris and Tokyo – a joyful photographic presentation. With a preamble about the Universe

21. From USA to Japan via Canada – A cheerful photographic documentary

22. 200 Wonderful Places, In The Last 50 Years – A personal photographic documentary

23. Must see places in USA and Japan - A kaleidoscopic photographic documentary

24. Grandeurs of the World - A kaleidoscopic photographic documentary

25. Corneliu Leu – writer on the same wavelength as Mark Twain. An American viewpoint

26. From Berkeley to Pompeii via Rome – A kaleidoscopic photographic documentary

27. From America to Europe via Japan - A kaleidoscopic photographic documentary

28. Discover America and Japan - A photographic documentary

29. J. R. Lucas – philosopher on a creative parallel with Plato, An American viewpoint

30. From America to Switzerland via France - A photographic documentary

31. From Bretton Woods to New York via Cape Cod - A photographic documentary

32. Splendid Places on the Atlantic Coast of the U. S. A. - A photographic documentary

33. Fourteen nice Cities on three Continents - A photographic documentary

34. 17 Picturesque Cities on the World Map - A photographic documentary

35. Unforgettable Places from Four Continents, including Trump buildings - A photographic documentary

36. Dediu Newsletter, Volume 1, Number 1, 6 December 2016 – Monthly news, review, comments and suggestions for a better and wiser world

37. Dediu Newsletter, Volume 1, Number 2, 6 January 2017 (available also at www.derc.com).

38. Dediu Newsletter, Volume 1, Number 3, 6 February 2017 (available at www.derc.com).

39. London and Greenwich, - A photographic documentary

40. Dediu Newsletter, Volume 1, Number 4, 6 March 2017 (available also at www.derc.com).

41. Dediu Newsletter, Volume 1, Number 5, 6 April 2017 (available also at www.derc.com).

42. Dediu Newsletter, Volume 1, Number 6, 6 May 2017 (available also at www.derc.com).

43. Dediu Newsletter, Volume 1, Number 7, 6 June 2017 (available also at www.derc.com).

44. London, Oxford and Cambridge, A photographic documentary

45. Dediu Newsletter, Volume 1, Number 8, 6 July 2017 (available also at www.derc.com).

46. Dediu Newsletter, Volume 1, Number 9, 6 August 2017 (available also at www.derc.com).

47. Dediu Newsletter, Volume 1, Number 10, 6 September 2017 (available also at www.derc.com).

48. Three Great Professors: President Woodrow Wilson, Historian German Arciniegas, and Mathematician Gheorghe Vranceanu – A chronological and photographic documentary

49. Dediu Newsletter, Volume 1, Number 11, 6 October 2017 (available also at www.derc.com).

50. Dediu Newsletter, Volume 1, Number 12, 6 November 2017 (available also at www.derc.com).

51. Dediu Newsletter, Volume 2, Number 1 (13), 6 December 2017 (available also at www.derc.com).

52. Two Great Leaders: Augustus and George Washington - A chronological and photographic documentary

53. Dediu Newsletter, Volume 2, Number 2 (14), 6 January 2018 (available also at www.derc.com).

54. Newton, Benjamin Franklin, and Gauss, A chronological and photographic documentary
55. Dediu Newsletter, Volume 2, Number 3 (15), 6 February 2018 (available also at www.derc.com).
56. 2017: World Top Events, But Many Little Known, A chronological and photographic documentary
57. Dediu Newsletter, Volume 2, Number 4 (16), 6 March 2018 (available also at www.derc.com).
58. Vergilius, Horatius, Ovidius, and Shakespeare - A chronological and photographic documentary.
59. Dediu Newsletter, Volume 2, Number 5 (17), 6 April 2018 (available also at www.derc.com).
60. Dediu Newsletter, Volume 2, Number 6 (18), 6 May 2018 (available also at www.derc.com).
61. Vivaldi, Bach, Mozart, and Verdi - A chronological and photographic documentary.
62. Dediu Newsletter, Volume 2, Number 7 (19), 6 June 2018 (available also at www.derc.com).
63. Dediu Newsletter, Volume 2, Number 8 (20), 6 July 2018 (available also at www.derc.com).
64. Dediu Newsletter, Volume 2, Number 9 (21), 6 August 2018 (available also at www.derc.com).
65. World History, a new perspective - A chronological and photographic documentary.
66. World Humor History with over 100 Jokes, a new perspective - A chronological and photographic documentary

Mathematical research papers published in international mathematical journals

1. Dediu, M. On the lens spaces. *Rev. Roumaine Math. Pures Appl*. **14** (1969) 623-627.

2. Dediu, M. Sur quelques propriétés des espaces lenticulaires. (French) *Rev. Roumaine Math. Pures Appl.* **17** (1972), 871-874.

3. Vranceanu, G; Dediu, M. Tangent vector fields in projective spaces V_3 and in the lens spaces $L^3(3)$. (Romanian) Stud. Cerc. Mat. **24** (1972), 1585-1600.

4. Dediu, M. Tangent vector fields on lens spaces of dimension three (Italian) *Atti Accad. Naz. Lincei Rend. Cl. Sci. Fis. Mat. Natur.* **54** (1974), no. 2, 329-334 (1977

5. Dediu, M. Campi di vettori tangenti sullo spazio lenticolare $L^7(3)$. (Italian) *Atti Accad. Naz. Lincei Rend. Cl. Sci. Fis. Mat. Natur. (8)* **58** (1975), no. 1, 14-17.

6. Dediu, M. Tre campi di vettori tangenti indepedenti sugli spazi lenticolari di dimensione $4n+3$. (Italian) *Atti Accad. Naz. Lincei Rend. Cl. Sci. Fis. Mat. Natur. (8)* **58** (1975), no. 2, 174-178.

7. Dediu, M. Sopra la metrica Vranceanu generalizzata (Italian) *Atti Accad. Naz. Lincei Rend. Cl. Sci. Fis. Mat. Natur. (8)* **58** (1975), no.3, 354-359).

8. Dediu, M. Sopra la metrica Vranceanu generalizzata (Italian) *Atti Accad. Naz. Lincei Rend. Cl. Sci. Fis. Mat. Natur. (8)* **58** (1975), no.3, 354-359).

9. Dediu, S.; Dediu, M. Sopra gli spazi proiettivi. *Rend. Sem. Fac. Sci. Univ. Cagliari* **46** (1976), suppl., 149-152.

10. Dediu, M.; Caddeo, Renzo; Dediu Sofia Alcune proprietà di una superficie immersa in uno spazio di Hilbert. (Italian) *Rend. Ist. Mat. Univ. Trieste* **8** (1976), no. 2, 147-161 (1977)

11. Dediu, S.; Dediu, M.; Caddeo, R. Alcune proprietà della metrica di Vranceanu generalizzata. (Italian) *Rend Sem. Fac. Sci. Univ Cagliari* **46** (1976), suppl., 153-161.

12. Dediu, Sofia; Dediu, M.; Caddeo, Renzo The Vrănceanu metric in local coordinates. (Italian) *Atti Accad. Sci. Lett. Arti Palermo Parte I (4)* **37** (1977/78). 331-339 (1980)

13. Dediu, M.; Caddeo, Renzo; Dediu, Sofia The extension of an *E*-premanifold to an *E*-manifold. (Italian) *Rend. Circ. Mat. Palermo (2)* **27** (1978), no. 3, 353-358.

Japan, Nikko, (140 km north of Tokyo): Toshogu Shrine, Japan's most lavishly decorated shrine, and the mausoleum of Tokugawa Ieyasu, the founder of the Tokugawa shogunate (1600-1850).

Michael M. Dediu is the editor of these books (also on Amazon.com, and www.derc.com):

1. Sophia Dediu: The life and its torrents – Ana. In Europe around 1920
2. Proceedings of the 4th International Conference "Advanced Composite Materials Engineering" COMAT 2012
3. Adolf Shvedchikov: I am an eternal child of spring – poems in English, Italian, French, German, Spanish and Russian
4. Adolf Shvedchikov: Life's Enigma – poems in English, Italian and Russian
5. Adolf Shvedchikov: Everyone wants to be HAPPY – poems in English, Spanish and Russian
6. Adolf Shvedchikov: My Life, My Love – poems in English, Italian and Russian
7. Adolf Shvedchikov: I am the gardener of love – poems in English and Russian
8. Adolf Shvedchikov: Amaretta di Saronno – poems in English and Russian
9. Adolf Shvedchikov: A Russian Rediscovers America
10. Adolf Shvedchikov: Parade of Life - poems in English and Russian
11. Adolf Shvedchikov: Overcoming Sorrow - poems in English and Russian
12. Sophia Dediu: Sophia meets Japan
13. Corneliu Leu: Roosevelt, Churchill, Stalin and Hitler: Their surprising role in Eastern Europe in 1944
14. Proceedings of the 5th International Conference "Computational Mechanics and Virtual Engineering" COMEC 2013
15. Georgeta Simion – Potanga: Beyond Imagination: A Thought-provoking novel inspired from mid-20th century events
16. Ana Dediu: The poetry of my life in Europe and The USA
17. Ana Dediu: The Four Graces
18. Proceedings of the 5th International Conference "Advanced Composite Materials Engineering" COMAT 2014
19. Sophia Dediu: Chocolate Cook Book: Is there such a thing as too much chocolate?

20. Sorin Vlase: Mechanical Identifiability in Automotive Engineering

21. Gabriel Dima: The Evolution of the Aerostructures – Concept and Technologies

22. Proceedings of the 6th International Conference "Computational Mechanics and Virtual Engineering" COMEC 2015

23. Sophia Dediu: Cook Book 1 A-B-C Common sense cooking

24. Sophia Dediu: Dim Sum Spring Festival

25. Ana Dediu and Sophia Dediu: Europe in 1985: A chronological and photographic documentary

Palazzo dei Conservatori (circa 1450, built on a Jupiter temple Maximus Capitolinus, from 550 BC), in Piazza del Campidoglio built by Michelangelo.